CONGO HEADMASTER

CONGO HEADMASTER

❖

The Story of an
African Adventure

HARRISON L. SHAFFER, JR.

with illustrations by the author

WHITEWING PRESS

San Francisco
1999

First printing 1999
Text and Illustrations
Copyright © 1999 by Harrison L. Shaffer, Jr.
All Rights Reserved

Published by
Whitewing Press
San Francisco, CA 94131-0319
Manufactured in the U.S.A.

Library of Congress Catalog Card No. 99-90409
ISBN 1-888965-00-2

PREFACE

THIS IS AN ACCOUNT of the experiences of my family and me during our adventure in the Belgian Congo from the time we left Spearfish, South Dakota, in June 1951 until we returned home in August 1957. This narrative was written for the children, so that they would know what we did when they were young.

It may also be of some interest for succeeding generations if they have any interest in family history. I have often wished that some of my ancestors had kept some record of their lives.

For most of the story I have relied upon my own memory but also made use of the letters we had written to our mothers who saved all of them. They were very helpful because they recalled events we had forgotten or added details to memories that had faded.

Information about the history and geography of Belgium and the Congo have been included because the story would not make much sense to anyone who has not visited those countries or at least read about them. The history of the Congo is particularly interesting because of the way it was discovered and developed.

I have taken the liberty of expressing my own opinions on several subjects. If anyone finds those passages tedious he can simply skip over them and go on to the rest of the story. I have tried to present an objective view of the Belgian administration which has in the past been unfairly maligned because of conditions existing at the time of the Congo Free State. I felt that someone should present an honest and objective picture of the administration by the Belgian colonial officers and colonialism in general, because we have been conditioned to believe that colonialism was inherently bad. I did not find it to be so.

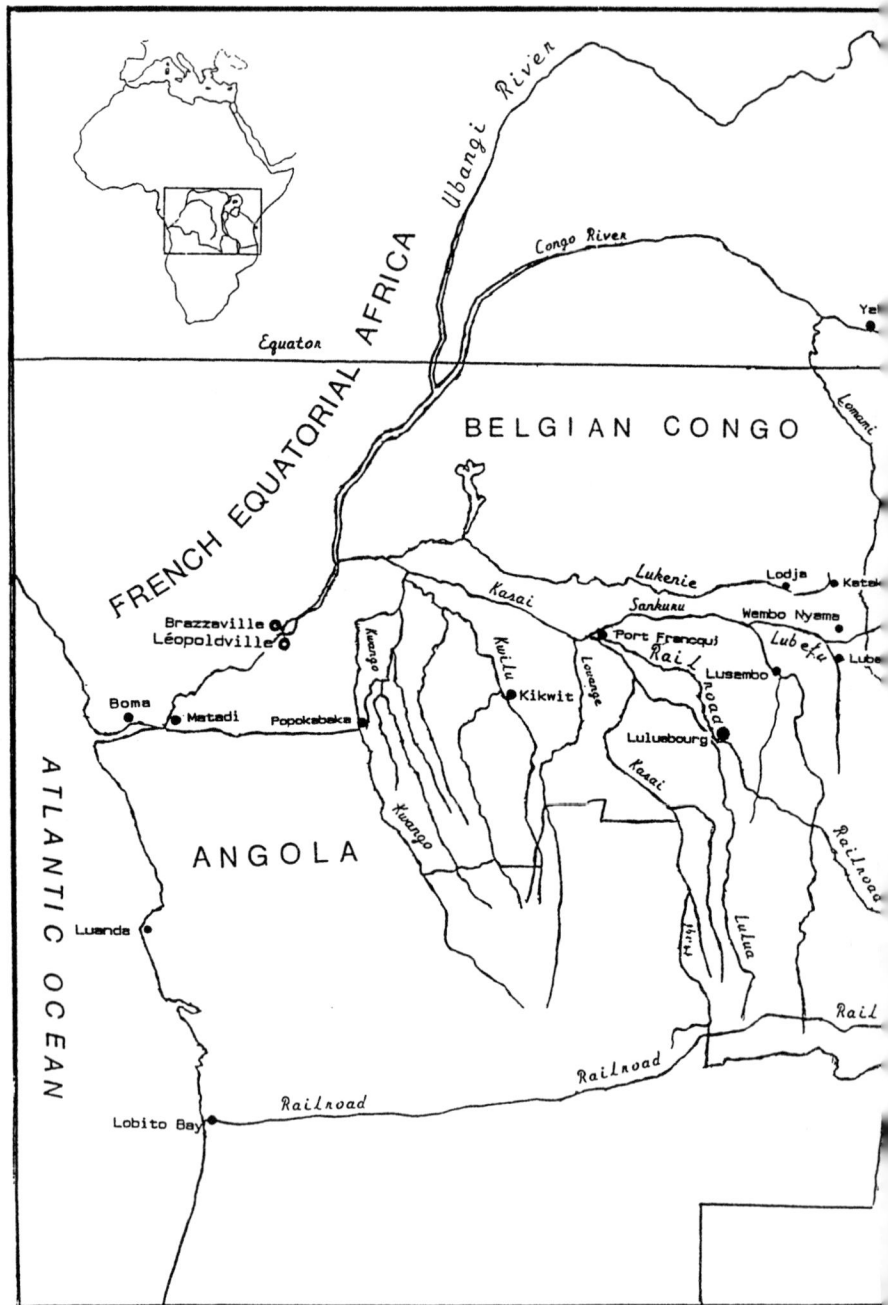

Ubangi River

Congo River

Ye[...]

FRENCH EQUATORIAL AFRICA

BELGIAN CONGO

Equator

Lomami

Lukenie

Lodja

Kasai

Sankuru

Katat[...]

Wembo Nyama

Brazzaville

Léopoldville

Port Francqui

Lubefu

Luba

Rai l

Kwango

Kwilu

Lusambo

Lulonga

road

Boma

Matadi

Popokabeka

Kikwit

Luluabourg

ATLANTIC OCEAN

ANGOLA

Kwango

Kasai

Railroad

Luanda

Brst

Lulua

Rail

Railroad

Rail

Railroad

Lobito Bay

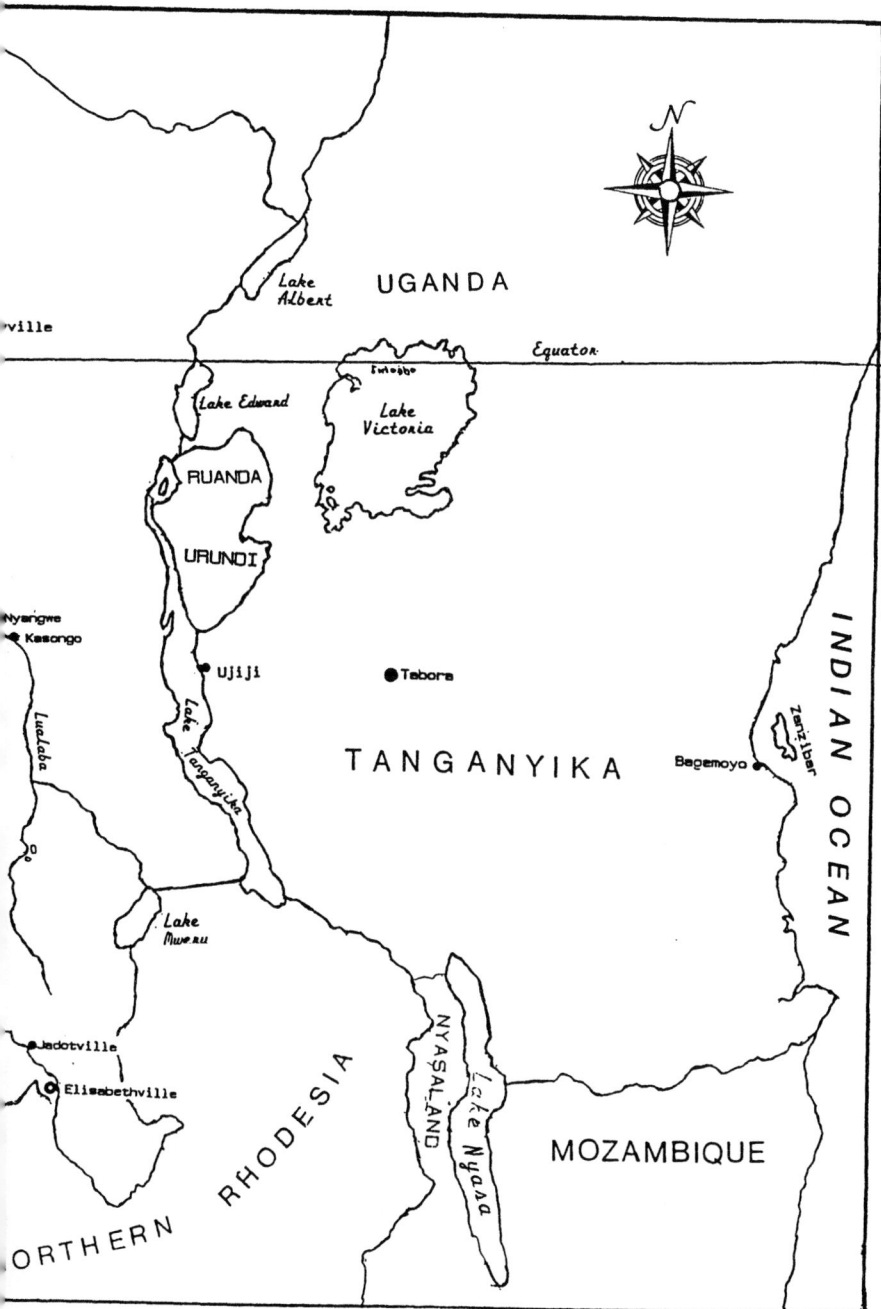

ville

N

Lake
Albert

UGANDA

Equator

Lake Edward

Lake
Victoria

Entebbe

RUANDA

URUNDI

Nyangwe
Kasongo

UJIJI

Tabora

TANGANYIKA

Lualaba

Zanzibar

Bagemoyo

INDIAN OCEAN

Lake Tanganyika

0

Lake
Mweru

Jadotville

Elisabethville

NYASALAND

Lake Ngasa

MOZAMBIQUE

ORTHERN   RHODESIA

CONTENTS

CHAPTER 1

We were teaching in Spearfish, South Dakota, and decided to look for something more challenging. The idea of teaching overseas had a strong appeal.

PROMPTED BY A SUGGESTION from an old friend, I have decided to try to put down some of the unusual experiences my family and I have had in strange places like Connecticut, Belgium, and the Belgian Congo. Some of them are experiences not everyone has had and some most people would just as soon not have, but a description of them might be entertaining and enlightening and might help others to understand what it is like to live in a culture very different from their own.

The best place to begin is Spearfish, South Dakota. When I finished my studies at the University of Denver in 1949, I could not find a job in my field—commercial art or advertising design—that paid enough to live on, so I considered teaching as an alternative. It was attractive because in theory it would give me time during the summer to paint or make pottery or pursue further studies. Fortunately, there was a shortage of qualified teachers, so finding a suitable position did not seem impossible. All I had to do was find a school district that was as desperate for a teacher as I was for a job, and that came together in Spearfish.

So we found ourselves in the Black Hills of South Dakota, my wife Jacqueline, our two sons, Harrison III and Paul, and me. I was teaching art and English in Spearfish Junior-Senior High School. The position did not pay very well, but we did manage and suffered no real hardship. Since I had no training in education—or to be more exact, pedagogy, the art and science of teaching—I was not well prepared to cope with the junior high English classes, but I did have some definite ideas about how to teach an art class with some content.

During the two years I was there neither the principal nor the superintendent ever visited my classes to see how I was doing. I found that strange, but apparently there were no complaints. Very few of the pupils showed much interest in learning, which was disappointing, and most of them seemed satisfied to become miners or ranchers as their fathers had done. I tried to convince them that writing and speaking English correctly was a worthwhile goal, but as one of the boys pointed out, his father, whose English was ungrammatical, earned more money than I did as a teacher, so my case was very weak. The art class had its difficulties, as it was held in a room used mostly for the business classes. The business teacher was very serious and very fastidious and naturally protested when we left the room in an unsuitable condition. I always apologized, but art can be a messy business.

Jackie had a few piano students and for one semester taught vocal music at Black Hills Teachers College (BHTC), which had formerly been called Spearfish Normal and has since been upgraded to Black Hills State University. It was ironic that I who had a master's degree and was theoretically qualified to teach in a college was teaching in a public school on an emergency certificate, and Jackie, who had the required teacher's certificate but lacked an advanced degree, was teaching in the college. It was an anomalous situation. She had been employed to deal with an emergency resulting from the sudden departure of the music teacher, who was suspected of selling some of the school's musical instruments and keeping the proceeds.

I painted signs part-time, so with what Jackie made we got along. During the summer I took courses at BHTC and some of them were very useful; the second year I was able to qualify for a teaching credential. Part of the summer I drove a dump truck in a rock quarry so could buy a better car.

The school district maintained a policy of hiring several new teachers from outside every year to supplement those who were Spearfish natives or who had found a home there. The experience was unpleasant for newcomers as the pupils seemed to delight in annoying the new teachers. None of them ever stayed more than two years, except for one English teacher who had found a comfortable niche. That most of the imported teachers left after two years was fine with the school board and the superintendent because beginning teachers were paid less, so hiring new teachers every year kept the school district's costs down.

There was one extraordinary aspect of the school: the music program. The music teacher was an elderly gentleman who had played in John Philip Sousa's band, in symphony orchestras, in vaudeville, in burlesque shows, in operas, and everywhere else. Having had a varied and interesting life he had settled in Spearfish to devote himself to training young musicians. Every student in the junior-senior high school who was interested in learning to play an instrument had a private lesson every week at no cost. Naturally, Spearfish High had an outstanding band for a school of its size.

During the summer we were there we enjoyed acting in the Black Hills Passion Play. Founded by Joseph Meyer, who had come from Germany, the play was presented three nights a week in an outdoor arena constructed for that purpose, and it was a spectacular sight. Almost everyone in town took part as volunteers, there not being all that much to do in the evening in Spearfish. It was a very good thing for Mr. Meyer, who played the part of Jesus, and for Spearfish. Jackie was one of the women in the crowd and I usually played one of the apostles. One night the man who usually played the part of the good thief was not there, and I was chosen to take his place and was crucified. I even had a line to say. I was terrified, but I did not forget my line.

Life in Spearfish was not bad. The people were kind and generous and the crime rate was close to zero. We never locked the front door from the time we moved in until the day we left, even during vacations. The winters were very harsh, with below zero temperatures much of the time. We lived in an old frame house that had no insulation, and the only sources of heat were a circulating gas heater in the dining room and the coal range in the kitchen for cooking. During the winter we kept a fire in the range and spent most of our time in the kitchen. The bathroom was unheated and taking a bath took real courage. The bedrooms too had no heat other than what drifted in from the dining room, and at times when it was thirty or forty degrees below zero outside, it would be ten below in the bedroom. After a while we seemed to adjust to the cold and did not mind it at all. I walked the few blocks to school every morning and we had our groceries delivered so we did not have to go out very much, and when we did we dressed warmly and were comfortable.

While we appreciated the beauty and the advantages of the Black Hills, we were city people and did not fit in in a rural community where the way of life was quite different from what we were used to. We would have always been outsiders. I did not feel that my ultimate destiny lay in Spearfish, so I started looking for an alternative. I thought about going back into the Air Force, but after some reflection I rejected the idea. Then one day I remembered that when I was in college I had met a fellow student who had been director of the ATC (Air Transport Command) band during the war. He told me that when the band was in India he had visited a place called Darjeeling where there was a missionary children's school. He described it as a virtual paradise, a beautiful place up in the mountains, away from the heat and humidity of the lowlands. I could see myself in a starched linen suit having tea on the verandah of a spacious bungalow like the characters in movies I had seen. I decided that it did seem attractive and appropriate now that I was a certified schoolmaster. The idea of traveling was appealing, and we would probably be able to save more money than we could in Spearfish. We were active members of the Methodist Church, so I went to see our pastor to ask him what he thought about the idea. His response may have been colored by his own secret desire to do some traveling, but he said he would encourage us to go ahead. After some protracted negotiations with the Methodist Board of Missions in New York we were hired, but instead of going to Darjeeling to teach American children we were to go to the Belgian Congo. When the personnel officer in New York learned that we spoke a little French—and it was very little—he decided it would be more appropriate to send us there to teach, not in a school for missionary children but in a teacher training school for Congolese natives.

That was acceptable because my experience in North Africa and Italy had aroused an interest in seeing more of the world, and I simply felt it was the right thing to do. Moreover, I had a strong feeling that life was too short to spend it sitting in one place. As it turned out, our motivation was not quite the same as most of the missionaries, whose main interest was saving souls. Our motives were more humanitarian, and it seemed to us that teaching in a foreign country would be interesting and worthwhile.

CHAPTER 2

*We leave Spearfish and travel by train to Hartford,
Connecticut, for a year of training to prepare us to
teach in the Belgian Congo.*

IN AUGUST 1951 we left Spearfish, went back to Denver for a
short time, and then went on to Hartford, Connecticut, for a
year of training. Travel in those days was more leisurely and in
some ways more pleasant than it is today.

We took the afternoon train to Chicago, leaving Denver
around five o'clock and arriving in Chicago the next morning
before breakfast. Instead of being crammed into narrow seats
without enough leg room, we had a spacious double bedroom
with wide, comfortable seats that were made up into beds at
night by the porter, and we had our own bathroom. We had
dinner in the dining car, where the food and the service—with
real china and real silverware—were superb and we watched
the countryside roll by as we ate. It is a shame that the people
who ran the railroads decided to get out of the passenger
business, because it used to be a very comfortable way to travel.

When we arrived in Chicago, we had to take a taxi from the
station to another station on the other side of the city, and once
we had checked our baggage we had the whole day to waste.
There was no way for the boys, who were four and two, to
have their naps, so we did our best to find things to do. It was
not a very satisfactory experience, however, so we were glad to
board the train for New York at five o'clock. We arrived in
New York the next morning, then went on to Hartford by
train and then to the school by taxi. here we moved into an
apartment on campus that had been reserved for us.

6

We spent the next nine months in the Kennedy School of Missions of the Hartford Seminary Foundation taking courses designed to prepare us for our work overseas. Jackie took most of the courses except that she took tropical hygiene and health instead of anthropology. The boys were in a well-organized preschool run by the wife of one of the professors. The courses included African culture, taught by a former missionary who had spent much of his adult life in Africa; anthropology; a course in Old Testament the first semester; and New Testament the second. There was no French class on campus, so we took French in a modern language school downtown. The course was taught by a Frenchman who worked in the post office during the day, and in spite of his lack of academic credentials, he was the best French teacher we ever had. He used an old book titled *French Without Toil* that was accompanied by records we listened to for hours in the evening. We can still remember words and phrases from that book.

I liked the course in religion because my knowledge of the Bible was rather scanty and because the course was taught by a scholarly professor of liberal tendencies who made it very interesting. My enthusiasm was not shared by the more conservative students, who seemed to feel the teacher was questioning their fundamentalist beliefs. That was my first face-to-face encounter with serious fundamentalists, and I could not understand their intolerance of those who did not agree with them. Theological disputes have never been one of my concerns, and I was sometimes amused by such discussions. I never expressed my own views, but one day I asked a young man who appeared to have very strong convictions how he could be so sure that he was right and all the others were wrong. He replied that he preached the gospel as it is. That ended the conversation. I avoided discussion of religion, but because I did not use the right clichés I had a problem.

The course in African culture was interesting because the

7

professor had so much experience upon which to draw and had such respect for Africans and their culture. It helped us to develop a positive attitude toward the people we were going to be working with on a basis of equality. The anthropology course was strange. It was taught by a little German professor who was amusing in a way, being somewhat pompous and dramatic. Knowing little about anthropology, I expected to be learning about Neolithic artifacts, pottery shards, and other aspects of material culture or such things as cranial measurements—always a big thing with anthropologists. Instead, we spent most of the semester studying beans, roosters, and snapdragons, all of which was nothing more than the study of Mendelian genetics. (You may recall that Gregor Mendel was a nineteenth-century Austrian monk whose experiments in cross-breeding plants and poultry over several generations established the basis for the science of genetics.)

The professor went into a great deal of detail to explain what happens when peas, snapdragons, and other flora with different characteristics are crossed. When it was all over and we had struggled with examination questions that seemed to bear no relation to the material covered in the lectures, I felt that a good instructor could have covered the same material in two or three weeks. The purpose of the exercise, which must have been very important to have taken so much time, was simply to convince everyone that there is no such thing as race in human beings. Toward the end the professor did discuss physical characteristics that are used to identify individuals as belonging to one race or another. He did make a good case for the lack of scientific basis for racial classifications and the belief that some races are superior to others.

The whole school had an intellectual and liberal slant, and there seemed to be a logical reason for using the Kennedy School of Missions to prepare missionaries for the field. Many of the missionary societies had to rely on the more conservative elements when recruiting, because such people were inclined to have the zeal that can be a strong motivating factor. Those same individuals might be the ones whose effectiveness would be enhanced by exposure to new ideas, which would help to broaden their perspective. It must have been successful much of the time, but in some cases the resistance was strong.

One day Bishop Booth, the Methodist bishop for central and southern Africa, came to Hartford to meet with all the Methodist missionaries who were going out. He was a very impressive person and we had a good meeting. He patiently answered many questions we had because we were going into a situation we knew very little about and one that was going to be very different from anything we had experienced before. The point I remembered, probably because I wanted to remember it, was that we were going there to meet the needs of the people. To me that justified our going. Bishop Booth told us there was great need for education in Africa to prepare for the future and we were going there to meet that need. There are those who would have said that we should leave those people alone and should not force our way of life upon them. I would have agreed with them except that "civilization" was going to come whether we liked it or not. If the people of Africa were going to be able to cope with the inevitable changes that were coming—President Kennedy's "Winds of Change"— they would be better off if they had some education to prepare them to handle their own affairs.

I realized later that many of the people we met in Hartford did not feel that was sufficient justification for going to Africa in the name of the church. They were going to do the Lord's work, as they put it, and to save souls. Some even felt they had been chosen by God to go to Africa and they may have been right. After listening to the bishop I was convinced that we were doing the right thing because the building of a church in Africa would require the skills of all kinds of people.

The second semester we took a course in linguistics taught by men who knew a lot about language, at least in theory. In the phonetics course the professor maintained that if one knows how a sound is produced physically and understands how the position of the lips, tongue, and other speech organs should be, one can produce the sound correctly. What he said was true in a sense, but he himself could not pronounce correctly the French words he used as examples. For me that emphasized the importance of the ear in the whole process, something he overlooked. The course was of great value because it did make us aware that American English uses only a fraction of the sounds it is possible to make with the human voice and that when speaking a foreign language one will communicate more successfully if he uses the sounds of that language rather than his own. That takes practice and concentration, which can be very tiring. Some of our friends developed very acceptable accents, while others continued to use only the sounds of their own American dialect because they could not hear the difference.

Later on, when we were learning an African language, our understanding of linguistics was very valuable; there are dimensions of the language that do not occur in English. For example, the length of a vowel can be phonemic—that is, it can be the means of distinguishing between two words. Also there were sounds we do not use at all, and the language was to some extent tonal, so being prepared to identify such elements was very helpful. There was one thing about the course that annoyed me. Almost like a daily prayer, or more aptly, an imprecation, the class would begin with an attack on grammarians, and all the books on linguistics pointed out very clearly what a bad influence they had on society. I do not believe I have ever seen a live grammarian, but from the linguists' descriptions they must all be miserable little monsters like the ogres in fairy tales, but with thick glasses and unpleasant personalities.

Neither the professors nor the authors of any of the textbooks would use any of the traditional terms such as *noun, verb,* or *adjective* because they were supposedly based on Latin. Instead, they went to absurd lengths to invent a whole new "scientific" vocabulary that was no more precise but did not have the stigma of having been used in traditional English classes. In a way this was a precursor of today's political correctitude.

At that time the science of linguistics was just getting on its feet, and it now appears that the scientific linguists have won the battle. The word linguist, by the way, does not mean someone who speaks several languages, and some of them do not speak any foreign language fluently. One who speaks several languages is a polyglot. To observe the results of the linguists' crusade that began in the early 1950s, all one has to do is listen to the radio or watch television. They have been successful in discrediting the grammarians, and they have managed to instill in future teachers the pernicious doctrine that one dialect is as good as another so there is no reason to try to teach grammar or syntax. As far as the linguists are concerned there is no such thing as standard English, and the idea that students should be taught to express themselves clearly, accurately, and possibly with style and originality is foreign to them. On the contrary, in parts of Los Angeles, for example, no attempt is made to correct what could be considered errors because this might interfere with the students' ability to retain the purity of their own dialect. The result is a disturbing number of functional illiterates. Supposedly the attempt to alter a person's natural way of expressing himself, inadequate though it may be, is discriminatory. Unfortunately, however, the ability to communicate effectively is considered important in the real world, and anyone who is not proficient in standard English is at a disadvantage.

At the end of the academic year we moved to New Haven for the summer to take an intensive French course at the

Institute of Far Eastern Languages at Yale University. The course was given there instead of in the regular French department because it was a special, serious course, using the most effective techniques of intensive language instruction. We were in class eight hours a day, which meant for the beginning students eight hours of concentrated drill and repetition. Although rote learning and memorization are considered old-fashioned and too demanding in today's schools, they are essential in serious language learning. Some of the beginning students who had not taken French previously almost broke under the pressure, but for most it was a very effective course.

Since I had already studied French and had paid attention during the year at Hartford, I was put in the advanced class, which was much easier and more interesting than the beginning class. Our instructor was a very unusual fellow. A German Jew, he had left Germany about 1939, had reached the United States just before the Second World War and had been drafted into the American army. He had not enjoyed his military service since most of his time was spent in a regiment that saw much action. He seemed rather bitter because it was obvious that his language ability should have been put to use. Having received a classical education as a child, he spoke German, Spanish, French, Latin, Greek, and Hebrew as well as English. He wanted to teach languages in a college or university, but in spite of his extraordinary ability he had to have a graduate degree to qualify, so he was paying his dues at Yale. In his master's thesis he quoted material in all the languages he knew and was cynically proud that there was no one on the Yale faculty who could read every language he had used.

We did a lot of reading in the class, mostly contemporary French fiction, and discussed the books in French. Existentialism, which I still do not understand, was in vogue with intellectuals so we had to read *L'Etranger* by Albert Camus and a collection of short stories by Jean-Paul Sartre, some of which were rather disgusting and hardly appropriate for that particular class. When one of the prim young ladies would object to the offensive subject matter the teacher would reply, *"Mais ça existe"* (But that exists). When one student asked him how to say "frustrated" in French, he shrugged his shoulders in a very French manner and replied, *"Cela n'existe pas en France"* (That does not exist in France). He seemed to enjoy tormenting the students. As it happens, with French the gestures are as important as the words themselves.

I got along well with this man, probably because I was different from the others, and at the end of the summer he gave me an A in the course. The dean marked it down to a B without knowing anything about me except that I was from somewhere in the great western wilderness and engaged in a profession that cast some doubt on my judgment. The grade did not matter to me, but it probably made the dean feel good to use his power, and it reinforced my observation that people in such institutions tend to be rather full of themselves.

While we were in Hartford we formed a close friendship with a couple from Ohio who were going to Algeria, perhaps the most difficult country on the African continent for a Christian missionary to work in. When we got to New Haven, we both had apartments on the third floor of an old building that belonged to the university. We had to share the kitchen so we found it convenient to have all our meals together. The other couple had two children about the same ages as ours, and we all got along wonderfully since we seemed to have a lot in common. It was very hot that summer and there was no air-conditioning, so we would go up on the roof to cool off.

By that time we had a good command of conversational French, just what we needed to get along in Brussels, and we were looking forward to trying it out. First we had to go to New York for a few days so after arranging for the shipment of our trunks and other heavy baggage we were on our way.

CHAPTER 3

We sailed from Hoboken, New Jersey to Antwerp,
Belgium, on an old freighter, went on to Brussels by
train, checked into a beautiful hotel, and started to
look for an apartment.

IN NEW YORK WE STAYED in an old hotel that might have been quite elegant at one time but had lost much of its charm. The best thing about it was its proximity to the Methodist Board of Missions. Getting around New York is not always easy for a stranger, as we found out when we had to go somewhere for yellow fever shots. After a final briefing in the office of the Board of Missions and confirmation of our shipping arrangements, we all took taxis to Hoboken, New Jersey, where the ship was docked. We noticed that the fare for the various parties varied from eight to twenty-one dollars, although we all left from the same hotel and went to the same dock. Because we had crossed the state line, we were at the mercy of the cab drivers, who were allowed to turn off their meters and charge whatever they thought they could get. We must not have looked too prosperous, because we paid only twelve dollars.

There were some tense moments before we embarked, because many of us had not yet had our passports returned from the Belgian consulate where they had been sent for visas. They finally did arrive and we were prepared for the thrills and excitement of a sea voyage. The ship we sailed on was the *Edam,* an old freighter the Holland-America Line did not feature in its advertisements. It was not that they were ashamed of it—and they had no reason to be, because in spite of its age it was clean and well maintained. As we sailed out of the harbor we passed the Statue of Liberty and the boys waved as we went by. It was an emotional experience.

The ship had no casino or swimming pool, but that was fine with us because all we wanted was a calm sea and plenty of time to do nothing. The absence of railings on most of the deck was a cause for concern because of the small children. Fortunately, there were several large oval life rafts on the deck, so we used one as a sort of playpen. Then someone who had made such a voyage before gave us a harness to put on Paul, our younger boy, so that he walked around on the deck like a pet dog on a leash when he was not confined to the life raft.

We were going cabin class, which we assumed would be less elegant than first class. It was comfortable but less than we were expecting. At least it was better than the so-called minimum first-class accommodations we had many years later on the *Lurline,* an American ship from Honolulu to San Francisco, because the cabins on the *Edam* at least had portholes. Jackie and the boys were in one cabin and I was in another with several other men. The sleeping arrangements did not matter because we spent most of our time on deck or in a small lounge reserved for cabin class passengers.

Across the corridor from our cabins was a small bar where every night some of the sailors who were being repatriated would gather to sing and play the guitar and drink up the money they had earned on American ships. There were about 150 of them in a sort of dormitory on a lower deck who had been caught working illegally on American ships and were being deported. One of the sailors told me that if he worked on a Belgian or Dutch ship he was paid eighty dollars a month, and if he did the same job on an American ship he made 500 dollars a month. That partly explains why the American merchant marine was dying. The sailors would sail to the United States on a European ship, jump ship, and work on an American ship until the immigration authorities caught up

Passing the Statue of Liberty was a very emotional experience.

Our accommodations could hardly be described as posh. However, the sailors at the bar outside our cabin were having a wonderful time.

with them and sent them back to Europe. They were a rough-looking bunch, but they were courteous and interesting to talk with.

The voyage was very pleasant. The weather was superb, the crew was friendly, and the food, though not fancy, was very good. The best part was sitting in a deck chair watching the sun go down over the water. After thirteen restful days we arrived in Antwerp, and after going through customs and immigration we took a train to Brussels. There we checked into a beautiful old hotel that was well kept and had a charm that was lacking in the hotel in New York. The first morning we made a big mistake. We ordered an American breakfast, complete with orange juice, bacon and eggs, toast, and coffee. It was very good but terribly expensive, since that is not the way things are done in Europe. From then on we ordered continental breakfasts, which were just as satisfying and much less costly.

While we were in the hotel we had several sessions with friends who were just finishing their year in Belgium and were ready to go to the Congo. Among them was a couple who were going out to teach in the same school we were headed for. After meeting them we were sure that we would like working with them. None of the other missionaries smoked or drank alcohol, but I could not help noticing that most of them made up for it by eating lots of sweets. As I am not addicted to sugar, and since I had given up smoking and agreed to observe the prohibition of alcohol, I felt it unfair that others could practice their vices and I could not. It seemed a shame to spend a year in the country that makes more varieties of beer than any other and not be able to benefit from it, but we had made a commitment and we stuck to it.

Someone announced that he was going out to buy some candy, preferably chocolates. One of the young ladies who had been there for a year warned that he should be careful because some of them contained brandy or some sort of liqueur, but that marzipan would be all right. I was impressed by the seriousness of her admonition. Not being particularly fond of anything sweet, I had never given much thought to chocolates with or without liqueur and had no idea how wicked eating such a confection was.

We had three days to find a place to live and no one to help us. There was someone who looked after such things as shipping and relations with the government for all the missionaries, a gentleman who spoke French fluently with a very solid British accent, but he did not have responsibility for lodging. There we were in a strange country, quite bewildered, and faced with the problem of finding an apartment in a short time. We bought some newspapers and started reading the classified sections. The first thing we learned was that a *pied-à-terre* was most likely a place more suitable for clandestine rendezvous than anything else. The ads for apartments were printed in the same sort of shorthand that is used in this country, where *frpl* stands for fireplace, except that in French the abbreviations are harder for a foreigner to understand. Although the prospect of trying to communicate by telephone in a foreign language was terrifying, we started calling. I was not only pleased but astonished to find that I was able to understand the people on the telephone, and even better, they could understand me.

We located several possibilities, then looked in our pocket guide to Brussels, a beautifully designed little booklet that had maps of every part of the city, to see where we were. I never went anywhere without my guide because it contained so much information about such things as tram and bus routes. We rented a Renault *quatre chevaux*, probably the smallest passenger car ever built, and proceeded to go out and look at apartments.

We finally found a comfortable and affordable apartment, our third third-floor walk-up since starting the adventure, at number 22 Avenue de la Renaissance. From our front windows we had a beautiful view of the vast park with its exquisite gardens, lawns, and trees and in the distance a huge arch like the Arc de Triomphe in Paris, complete with bronze horses on top. A boulevard ran through the arch and on one side was a huge museum filled with all kinds of weapons, military uniforms, and other paraphernalia, including a metal cot used by Napoleon during his many campaigns. On the other side was the Museum of Art and History, also a large structure with all sorts of paintings and sculpture and a fine library.

Across the street were a bicycle path and tracks for a tram that came by frequently and made it possible for us to get around without owning a car. Shopping was easy because there were plenty of small shops of all kinds within a few blocks. We moved into the apartment, which was furnished with what would be considered antiques in the United States, but we did not get completely settled for two weeks because our trunks had been sent to Amsterdam or Rotterdam instead of being unloaded in Antwerp. The custom of misdirecting baggage is an old tradition, going back to well before air travel became popular.

The building was what was called a *maison de ville*, or what we would call a townhouse, originally intended for one family. In Brussels, Paris, and other European cities most people live in similar three- or four-story buildings with an attic and a mansard roof. The landlady and her mother occupied the ground floor and each of the upper floors had been turned into an apartment. In the front of the apartment were the living room and kitchen. The massive dining room table with carved chairs was in one end of the living room and there was a small table in the kitchen that served well for breakfast and lunch. The ceilings were very high, and the French doors, almost as high as the ceiling, opened out onto a small balcony. The red velvet drapes went well with the heavy carved furniture and added to the air of permanence and stability of the building.

Behind the living room, in the middle of the apartment, was a large bedroom we used and behind that was the room where the boys slept and played. It too had a small balcony that overlooked the back garden that was enclosed by a high brick wall. The bathroom was large, with white tile on the floor and walls and a large bathtub with a strange water heater. The heater only went on when the hot water tap was turned on. It then came on with a sort of explosion that was scary until we got used to it. It was very efficient and saved a lot of gas. Above the apartment was an empty garret, similar to the one in *La Bohème,* that would have made a wonderful studio.

CHAPTER 4

*We adjust to life in Brussels. The boys enroll in the
neighborhood school and start to learn French. We
learn about the Belgian welfare system.*

ONCE WE HAD MOVED IN we had to have something to eat, so
I did something that may seem cruel. I thought that the sooner
Jackie learned to shop the better, so I told her she would have
to go shopping. I would have liked to go with her, but someone had to stay with the boys, so I gave her a handful of francs
and gently pushed her out the door. She was in tears, but after
all, grocery shopping was going to be her responsibility, and
besides, I knew she could do it without any trouble. Half an
hour later she came back with the groceries and was very proud
of her accomplishment.

For the first few months the weather was beautiful, with
pleasant temperatures and very little rain, so we spent much of
our time in the parks, either taking long walks or riding our
bicycles along the bicycle paths. Then in October it began to
cool and on October 15 our rent went up substantially to cover
the cost of central heating. The custom in Europe was that the
central heating went on October 15 and was turned off April
15, regardless of the weather. In our apartment we did not
notice any difference and we referred to the *chauffage central* as
chômage central—the word *chômage* meaning "unemployed"—
since the radiators seldom emitted any heat at all.

From October until April it was quite cold most of the
time—not an invigorating dry cold followed by mild weather
and sunshine such as we have in Colorado but a steady,
depressing, relentless chill that was aggravated by a frequent

drizzle and a continually overcast sky. I wondered how Rubens and the great Flemish masters managed to turn out such magnificent paintings when it was so dark much of the year. How did they see to work? In an effort to keep warm we built fires in a little stove that was plugged into the fireplace in the living room, using coal we bought in small sacks at the grocery store. It was not entirely satisfactory because the coal did not burn very well, probably because the chimney had not been cleaned for years.

When the cold became intolerable, we would go into the kitchen, light the oven in the gas stove, and huddle around it in sweaters and sometimes overcoats. Many evenings I sat at the dining room table in an overcoat and gloves trying to do my homework. The bedrooms had no heat at all, but we did have wonderfully thick comforters so that once we got into bed we were quite comfortable. We were told that there was a bar or café for every thirty-three people in Belgium, which seemed like a lot, but considering the heating situation, I surmised that a lot of people spent the evening drinking beer in a cozy café until it was time to go to bed, then rushed home and slipped under the comforters.

We replaced the standard forty-watt light bulbs with sixty-watt bulbs in some of the rooms so we could see at night, and we used enormous amounts of gas, for which we were allowed to pay, of course. We used so much gas that we put the entire building in a higher category, which displeased Mademoiselle, our landlady, greatly. The Belgians were way ahead of us when it came to conservation. At that time the word was not even in our vocabulary. The more gas a person used, the higher the rate he had to pay so that people were encouraged to conserve, because Belgium did not have huge reserves of gas that some-one wanted to sell. One day Mademoiselle told me that we took entirely too many baths so we did our best to conform by bathing less frequently. Of course, if she had provided the heat we were paying for we would not have been obliged to use so much gas. The landlady and her mother, whom we called Madame, were not bothered by the cold because they lived in a sort of *sous-sol*, a semi-basement, and kept a fire going in a coal range the way we had done in Spearfish. They leased the house from the owner so they had a place to live and a small income from the rental of the two upper floors.

During the year we lived at 22 Avenue de la Renaissance there were three other tenants in the second-floor apartment. First there was a junior Polish diplomat and his wife who appeared to be desperately poor. They had bought a record player, but they seemed to have only one record that they played over and over. We assumed that they had bought the phonograph to take back to Poland since such luxuries were difficult to find there because of the destruction caused by both the Germans and the Russians. They never spoke to us, probably because we were considered enemies by their government.

The Poles left after a few months and did not seem pleased to be going home. They were followed by a retired Belgian general and his domineering wife, whom Mademoiselle called Madame la Générale. In some countries it is the custom to refer to the wife of a high-ranking officer in that way, but in this case it was obvious who gave the orders. The general himself was very pleasant and seemed resigned to his condition. They were there only a few months and then were replaced by a British family. The father was in Belgium as a salesman representing a tile manufacturer. They were a much happier bunch than either of their predecessors and the only ones we had any contact with at all.

There was no refrigerator in the apartment since at that time most Europeans managed to do without them, but we were Americans and we thought we ought to have one because we were not accustomed to putting perishable food on the

24

Brussels seemed to have a policeman, or agent, on every corner and hardly any in patrol cars. They were always very helpful.

The natives could always spot American tourists. Even when I wore a black beret they could always tell I was American.

windowsill. Their system obviously worked; it was just that we were not used to it. We discussed the problem with Mademoiselle and agreed that if she would buy a small refrigerator, and it was very small, we would make the monthly payments. So we paid five dollars a month, and when we left she had an electric refrigerator, quite a luxury at that time.

I am not sure whether it was the climate, which was cold and damp, or anxiety caused by fear of the unknown and the uncertainty concerning my chances of surviving in an environment where I did not quite fit in, but Jackie came down with pneumonia. Mademoiselle called a kindly old doctor who examined her frequently and charged 200 francs a visit, which was about four dollars. After he examined her he always told her, *"Ne pas s'inquiéter, ne pas s'énerver, ça ira,"* which means "Don't get excited, don't be nervous, everything is going to be all right." He was wise and understood the cause of her illness and treated it successfully by his reassurance and a minimum of drugs. He prescribed a heart stimulant, some vitamin B-12, and a glass of red wine every day to fortify the blood.

He also arranged for a visiting nurse to come frequently to treat Jackie with *ventouses*, which are small glass suction cups. She would heat the suction cups, have Jackie lie down on her stomach and apply the cups to her back to draw the blood to the surface. It was an old-fashioned method, but it seemed to work. We were not supposed to drink any kind of alcoholic beverages because of our commitment to total abstinence. However, we felt that since Jackie's life was at stake, we should obey the doctor's orders. I did not want her drinking alone and believed that if it did her that much good it would also be good for me, so we quietly had our glass of red wine until she got well.

Because of her illness and the need for her to rest as much as possible, we hired a young Flemish girl to come in several days a week to help with the housework. We did not have to pay her very much because she was only there part-time, which was good because we did not have much money. She did say, however, that if she could have lunch on the days she came that would be appreciated. We thought it was a good idea, especially since she would prepare the meals on those days. We had an introduction to authentic Flemish cooking, including the famous national dish, *carbonnade flamande*, which we liked very much. The only problem was that she ate twice as much as the rest of us combined on those days, making it her main meal of the day.

Marie was a good worker and very friendly. One day she took us out to Hal, a village about fifteen miles from Brussels, to her mother's farm. It was like going back 100 or 200 years in time. It was the sort of experience few tourists ever have. Everything looked so old. The horse, the cow, and the pigs lived in a barn that was attached to the house, an arrangement that seemed to be popular on European farms but has never caught on in the United States. There was also a vicious-looking dog chained in the front yard, suggesting that there might be a security problem.

Several people drove by in horse-drawn carriages, which seemed to be the usual form of transportation in the country. We visited the local church and saw the elaborately dressed figure of the Black Virgin, which was the object of veneration and considered to be sympathetic to supplications from the faithful. The Belgians are very Roman Catholic and although attendance at Sunday church services is less than what the church authorities would like, religious ceremonies seem to be very popular. For example, the day we visited Hal, the church with the image of the Black Virgin was crowded.

It was either Mardi Gras, the last day before the beginning of Lent and the last day that meat can be served before the forty-day period of abstinence, or *mi-carême*, a day in the middle of Lent when the rules are temporarily relaxed so that

*The parade in Hal was an exciting spectable. There was
such a crowd that it was difficult to get good photographs.*

The visit to Bruges was one of the highlights of our stay in Belgium.
It was such a beautifully preserved medieval city.

people can enjoy themselves for a day, and they did. Included in the big parade in Hal were the Gilles de Binche, from the village of Binche. The men wore elaborate costumes, which we were told dated back to the sixteenth century and were inspired by the costumes of the Aztecs at the time of the Spanish conquest. At that time the Low Countries, Belgium and Holland, were part of the Hapsburg Austrian Empire, which also included Spain. Some of the men from Binche were on stilts and wore grotesque masks as they advanced in a distinctive shuffling gait. The whole parade was quite impressive.

On Good Friday there was no school, so we all went to Bruges to see the annual parade. Bruges was a remarkable city. It had been an important port until the estuary silted up and prevented easy navigation. Visiting Bruges was like going back in time, because most of the buildings were hundreds of years old and still in excellent condition. The Belgians respect the past and do take care of their architectural heritage. That day in Bruges there was a parade, or pageant, that lasted all day long. Floats and tableaux told the story of the Bible beginning with Genesis. With the medieval architecture, narrow streets, canals, and so many people dressed in the costumes they wore in the procession, we felt we were having an experience that would be impossible to duplicate anywhere else.

The boys were three and five when we arrived in Brussels, so we put them in the nearby primary school, which included kindergarten and preschool. The school was enclosed by a high wall with a large, heavy door. It was a very serious looking place. Neither boy spoke French, and the teacher did not speak English, or if she did she did not use it. At first the boys just sat in the corner and listened, but within a few weeks they began to communicate, and by the end of the school year they spoke French nearly as well as English. Our older boy went so far as to say that he preferred French because it was more beautiful. They did not want to speak French with us but used it freely with Belgians. They adapted easily to Belgian customs, including using the flannel slippers Mademoiselle insisted that they wear so as not to disturb those in the apartment below.

At that time the Belgians had a very efficient day-care system. Any woman who worked could take her children to a very well run day care center with a professional staff and very good facilities, leave them there, and pick them up after work, confident that they had been well cared for and fed. We are now only beginning to discuss solutions to problems they solved more than fifty years ago.

One day Hari, as we called our oldest son, fell down the wrought iron stairs leading into the garden and we thought he had broken his elbow. We took him to what was called the American hospital, a hospital that had been built and endowed by some Americans after the First World War. He was examined by several doctors who, upon seeing the X-rays, decided that his arm was not broken but that he would need therapy, so we took him to the hospital several times a week. We had no health insurance, but it did not matter because each visit to the hospital, including the first consultation and the X-rays was only forty francs, or about eighty cents.

Shopping in Brussels was an interesting experience and one that allowed us to have contact with people, which was necessary if we were to learn their language and customs. Often there would be no one else in the shop so we would have time to chat with the shopkeeper and practice our French. While in Spearfish we had been able to have our groceries delivered and had been accustomed to going to a supermarket for most of our groceries elsewhere; in Brussels it was different. There were two large stores downtown that were almost like supermarkets, but most of our purchases were made in small, specialized shops in the neighborhood. The only thing we really had to go downtown for was peanut butter, which was sold in small jars in the delicatessen section along with items such as anchovies and caviar. We did like going downtown for other reasons. There were so many interesting sights to see, elegant shops and department stores, some with tea rooms where shoppers could relax with some light refreshments and listen to a string quartet in a genteel atmosphere.

When we thought we could afford it, we also liked to go to the Métropole for coffee. It was the most elegant hotel in Brussels and the most expensive, but the service in the coffee shop was exceptional and available to anyone. If someone wanted to experience what it was like to belong to the nobility for an hour or so it was the place to go. The waiters all wore full dress suits and white gloves and the coffee was served in individual filters on little tables surrounded by couches and armchairs. Toward the end of our stay in Brussels we went to the Métropole one evening for dinner. It was wonderful and something we remembered for a long time. Ordinarily, if we went out for dinner at all we went to a store called Sarma that was like Woolworth's and served a steak with salad and French fries for under a dollar.

We had some friends who lived in a *pension* that was noted for the quality of its cuisine. It was in a beautiful big house with a garden that included a small greenhouse where the landlady raised grapes. Belgium is too far north to have much of a wine industry, but Belgians do raise marvelous grapes called *raisins de serre* in greenhouses. Every time we went there the main course was rabbit. The landlady had a shotgun and a ferret, and every Saturday she would go hunting. When she found a rabbit's hole she would turn the ferret loose and he would dive into the warren. When the rabbits came out the other end, she would blast several of them for her guests to have for Sunday dinner. Rabbit is delicious when properly prepared and is very popular in Europe.

We did most of our shopping in a small *épicerie* owned by a couple who were true Bruxellois. It was there that we bought fresh produce, staples, canned goods, and coal for the stove. Every morning about two o'clock the husband would go down to the central market and select each piece of fruit and each vegetable personally, so that everything in his shop would be absolutely first class. He would return about six, arrange the day's selection and then go back to bed. His wife would run the store until he had had his nap. Then he would be there until closing time. Of Flemish origin, the couple had always lived in the city and spoke both French and Flemish without scrupulous attention to the grammar and syntax of either. They did, however, manage to communicate very well and were among the nicest people we met in Belgium.

One day when there was no one else in the store, the grocer motioned me over to a corner and in a low voice said that he had a question. He had several ears of corn and asked me what they were and what one would do with them. I explained that it was American corn and told him how we would prepare it. I bought all the corn he had, which was not much, and he seemed relieved. I believe some corn was raised for animal feed, but at that time it was not usually served to people. Mr. Van Aerschot, the grocer, took a personal interest in his customers. A few days later Jackie came home after doing her shopping and found some onions she had not bought. When she asked him about them the next day he said that he had assumed that she had just forgotten to ask for them and so he put some in. Onions are very important in the Belgian diet.

Both Jackie and I had tutors for French, but since I was doing quite well in that language I had my tutor give me lessons in Flemish, using French as the medium of instruction. I was curious and wanted to learn a little Flemish too, but it was more difficult than I thought it would be. I did learn to count and learned the names of the vegetables and some other groceries and the vocabulary for shopping so I could do much of my shopping in Flemish. That delighted Mr. Van Aerschot.

This picture is not accurate, as Jackie spoke French so well that no one had trouble understanding her. Rather, it represents the fear we had before going shopping.

Shopping for groceries was one of the most interesting things we did. I always had to remember to take my filet to carry things home in.

For beef we went to a butcher shop a few doors away from the grocery store, a one-man operation where the butcher would buy a side of beef or whatever he thought he would need for that day and prepare it himself. The meat was always fresh and of fine quality. He did not use a meat grinder and if we wanted ground beef he would chop it up with a cleaver. He was a purist and felt that using a meat grinder would compromise his principles. Another shop, called a *charcuterie*, sold nothing but pork, which received the same personal attention as did the beef in the butcher shop. The pork butcher also made fresh pâté every day, as well as his own well-seasoned, delicious sausage. For fruit we sometimes went to a third store that specialized in cheese. On Fridays the *poissonerie*, which was closed most of the week, would open and sell fresh fish. Our bread came from a bakery around the corner and it was always fresh and wholesome. If we had it sliced, the baker put it in a waxed paper bag that cost fifty centimes the first time and was supposed to be reused.

Except for the baker with his bag for sliced bread, none of the merchants had bags for groceries. Potatoes and similar items were wrapped in yesterday's newspaper and each shopper was expected to carry a strong string bag called a *filet* in which to carry purchases home. If I did happen to buy some things on the way home from school I would drape the filet over the handlebars of my bicycle and pedal serenely home without attracting attention.

CHAPTER 5

*A little Belgian history. A description of the French
class. We visit Paris. The examination system.*

TO UNDERSTAND HOW BELGIUM came to be what it is today,
a brief look at history is useful. Belgium had the misfortune of
not only being a bilingual country but also of being the victim
of religious differences. For centuries it had been ruled by the
Hapsburgs, so after the abdication of Charles V, who had been
born in Ghent and was a true European, control passed to
Philip II, King of Spain. That happened during the Refor-
mation. Those who were Protestants revolted against the
oppressive rule of King Philip, a fanatical Catholic, and moved
to Holland, which became a Protestant republic. Those who
wished to remain Catholic and loyal to the king stayed in what
is now Belgium.

In 1815 at the Congress of Vienna, which took place after
the defeat of Napoleon for the purpose of organizing European
affairs, Belgium and Holland were united in one country with
a Dutch king. The king, William I, was a Protestant and
unwisely began to close monasteries and persecute Catholics.
As a result, the 1830 revolution in France spilled over into
Belgium and led to an uprising in Brussels in August. The
intransigence of King William led to a complete break and the
proclamation of Belgian independence in October.

The outcome was a country where the people in the north
spoke Flemish and those in the south, known as Walloons,
spoke French and their own dialect. There were and still are
some cultural differences, but the Belgians are to be admired
for way they have generally been able to resolve the resulting

The gargoyles on European churches are beautifully grotesque and serve as water spouts and to repel evil spirits.

Even when it is quite chilly, people can be seen having their coffee or apéritif on the terrace of a café.

problems peacefully. The question of who the leader should be was resolved by bringing in someone who was neither a Fleming nor a Walloon. Léopold, a German prince from the Duchy of Saxe-Cobourg-Gotha became Léopold, King of the Belgians. There is a subtle difference between being the King of the Belgians and being the King of Belgium. The kings have generally been popular in Belgium and as a symbol of unity have held the country together.

I first became aware of what an emotional issue the language problem was when I saw a poster in Flemish announcing a course in African art at the Museum of Art and History. Since I was interested in learning as much as I could about African sculpture, I went to the museum and told the young lady at the reception desk that I would like to take the course. It was to be given one afternoon a week for six weeks and it would be possible for me to fit it into my schedule.

She told me that she would have to ask the curator of African art, so she called him and he came down to meet me. I told him that it was essential for me to take the course because I was going to Africa and hoped to become a collector. Because it was such a great opportunity I was surprised that I was the only person who had shown an interest in the class. He told me in French that he was sorry but the course was being offered in Flemish. I replied that I did not care what language it was given in and that it was so important to me that I was sure I would learn something from it.

He finally agreed to let me take the course, so I paid the modest fee and every Thursday afternoon I went to his office for a visit. First he would take me through the fine collection of African sculptures on display and would then proceed to give the series of lectures he had prepared, all in Flemish. The lectures were actually notes he had prepared for a guide to the museum's collection that he was writing. The collecting included objects from every African country except the Belgian

Congo. All the art from the Congo was in the Congo Museum at Tervueren, and a fine collection it was, because the Belgian anthropologists had a sincere appreciation of the art of the Congo.

The curator lectured first in Flemish and then, since he spoke both French and English fluently, he would translate what he had said into one of those languages. We became very good friends and long after the projected six weeks had passed I was still going to the museum for his lectures, which were always in Flemish with a following translation. That the lectures be given in Flemish was for him a matter of national pride.

One day we had the curator over to our apartment for lunch. After lunch he picked up my guitar and began to play a song that is a sort of national anthem of the Afrikaners, the original white settlers in South Africa. He sang it with strong emotion, in Afrikaans, and I realized that the Flemish, or at least some of them, identified strongly with the Afrikaners, most of whom were originally Dutch or Flemish and probably Protestant. The Afrikaners were persecuted by the British and many Flemish felt they had been badly treated by the Walloons, so there was a certain amount of empathy.

I also spent as much time as I could at the Congo Museum and got to know some of the anthropologists who worked there. They were active in all kinds of research, including the collection and study of sculpture and other arts, language studies, and recordings of the music of the various tribes. Because of their interest in the art of the Congo it was difficult even that early to find a good piece; the Belgian anthropologists and others had gone through the country with great thoroughness. That was fortunate, because they preserved much magnificent sculpture that otherwise would have been lost; since the local people had lost interest in it and wooden objects do not survive long in a tropical climate unless they are taken care of. All the people I met in the museums were very kind to me and did everything they could to help me to learn. Most of the staff in the Congo Museum were Flemish. The director, an outstanding scholar, had written the most comprehensive book on the art of the Congo, but in Flemish, and up to that time he had not allowed anyone to translate it. It was good that I was able to study the art of Africa and especially the Congo, as it enabled me to become fairly knowledgeable so that I might do some collecting and know what to look for.

One day Dr. Wyns, the curator, invited us out to his house in the country for lunch. It was a house he had built recently in the traditional style of Flemish farmhouses, with tiles and beams he had collected dating back as far as the sixteenth century. What impressed me most was the thatched roof, which was about a foot thick. Never having seen a thatched roof, I asked him how long it would last. He replied that the north side was guaranteed only for fifty years, but the south side would probably last forever. It was made of reeds that grow in that area and was treated to make it fireproof.

In late September school started. Although the tramway was quite efficient, I often rode my bicycle instead; it was pleasant to ride along the bicycle path. Every morning at eight o'clock I reported to the Colonial School on the Avenue Louise, in an elegant part of the city several miles from where we lived. The building was said to have been the residence of a princess who was related to the Emperor Napoleon. The first day all the students were assembled in a large room and were given a placement test consisting of a *dictée*, or dictation. It was a very simple and accurate way to evaluate each student's level of proficiency. I missed only one word, one which I took to be *pain*, which means bread, instead of *pin*, which means pine. I wondered what bread was doing waving in the wind, but I was not familiar with the word for pine and wrote down what I heard.

The professor, Gilsoul by name and a former army officer, immediately divided the class into two groups according to ability, and I was in the advanced class. He then divided the class into squads or teams and put a leader, called a *chef d'équipe,* in charge of each one. Because I had made only one mistake on the *dictée,* I was the leader of my team. He also appointed an Englishman named Bertie the leader of the entire class, sort of a first sergeant. The class needed some sort of organization, because it was large, about fifty-two students from at least half a dozen countries. No English was spoken, because many of the students were from countries where English was not the national language. When the professor wanted someone to answer a question, he would never call upon an individual student but would ask one of the team leaders to choose someone to answer the question. It was a system that worked very well with motivated adult students from varied backgrounds.

During the year the emphasis was on grammar, syntax, and phonetics rather than on conversational ability. After all, many of us were going to be teaching French, following an academic curriculum, so it was knowledge most of us would find very useful later on. Professor Gilsoul found out somehow that I could draw, so when we had our weekly lesson on phonetics, he would have me go to the blackboard and make a drawing of the position of the tongue and so forth, to illustrate it for the other students while I gave them a description I had memorized from the book on phonetics. My drawings were always accurate because I copied them out of a very serious treatise on phonetics we had been advised to add to our library. I had no idea how much the other students got out of it, but I learned a lot about phonetics, which was important because French-speaking people like to have their language pronounced properly. They do not find foreign accents "cute" as we do.

The course was very academic for the reasons cited and

covered all the grammar that a student in a college preparatory school would be expected to master. There seemed to be undue emphasis on obscure exceptions to many of the rules we were learning, such as the two plural forms of the word *ciel,* meaning sky, which varies according to whether one is talking about real skies (*cieux*) or skies in paintings (*ciels*).

We spent many hours learning all the rules and becoming proficient in the analysis of sentences and clauses. Then at the end of the year, I happened to look at the appendix of the huge grammar book, *Le Bon Usage,* and found that according to a 1949 decree, much of what we had been learning was not required any more. Later on when I was teaching French in the Congo I was glad that I did have such a thorough knowledge of the language.

One day we had a valuable lesson in the danger of false cognates, of which there are many because about forty percent of the words in modern English come from French. A cognate is a word that is spelled the same, or nearly so, in two languages but does not necessarily have the same meaning in both of them. A false cognate is one that does not. For example, in English the word sensible means having good common sense; *sensible* in French means sensitive. A young lady—who appeared to be without blemish to such an extent that she could have cast the first stone—submitted a short essay in which she use the word *luxurieusement,* which certainly sounds like the word luxurious, to say that missionaries do not live that way. Mr. Gilsoul burst out laughing as he read it and said that of course it was true since the word did not mean luxuriously but rather lewdly or lustfully. The word she wanted was *luxueusement,* which does mean luxuriously and is the source of our term deluxe. He may have been a little heavy-handed but it did make us all aware of the danger of false cognates. He also told us that whenever we write anything we should have a dictionary handy and use it.

The French class lasted until noon, with a long break in the middle so the British students could have their morning tea. We Americans usually made do with a cup of coffee from a thermos during the ten o'clock break. The British, on the other hand, brought out huge hampers with all sorts of scones and biscuits and other items one has with morning tea. What was for us a short break was for them a formal ritual and a rather pleasant one. I wondered, though, how they managed to carry all that on a bicycle.

There were other differences between us and the British. While most of us did not consider ourselves terribly well off, compared to them we were positively affluent. Most of them were shabbily dressed, all the men wearing threadbare tweed jackets with leather patches on the elbows and the women looking as plain as possible. I was told that the elbow patches were put on after the elbow had worn through in order to render useful a venerable garment. To this day I find the sight of a new jacket with elbow patches objectionable, because according to tradition the patches have to be earned and worn only on old jackets.

Jackie was not enrolled in the Colonial School but studied with a tutor and was free to do whatever interested her. Being a musician and a singer, she joined the *Grande chorale protestante*, a very professional group organized by a Protestant minister who was also an accomplished musician. The Protestant church in Belgium was very small, and in some parts of the country still subject to some persecution, but it did exist and the *chorale* was highly respected. They put on quite a few concerts that were well attended because it was the best choral group in the country.

In the same group were two individuals who stood out from the rest. One was Bertie, our leader in the French class, who was also a serious musician and singer. Then there was Meg, a slightly plump and dowdy young woman with a very

46

ruddy complexion and an obvious determination to go to the
Congo as a missionary and also to do so as Bertie's consort. For
some obscure reason she developed an antipathy to Jackie,
probably because Jackie was more attractive and more talented
than she was, and because she was American as well, which
sometimes is enough in itself. One day she told Jackie, "You
know, your husband could pass for a Scot but you look terribly
American." I took it as a compliment that confirmed a suspi-
cion I have always had, that I must have had Scottish or Celtic
ancestors of some kind because of the way I thrill to the sound
of the bagpipes.

I could not imagine why Meg had such a strange attitude
toward Jackie, who would not have done anything to offend.
She is one of the kindest and most gentle people I have ever
known. Meg also told Jackie that wearing that lipstick and with
that "eye" she could easily get into trouble. Meg was probably
successful in snaring Bertie, and I am sure she saved many
erring Africans from perdition. We never saw or heard of them
again after leaving Belgium because the Congo is a big place,
three times as big as the state of Texas.

Joining the chorale was the best thing Jackie could have
done. Both the British and the mainland Europeans have terms
for musical notation that are quite different from those used in
the United States. The British have a quaint system in which
what we call a whole note is a semibreve, a quarter note is a
crochet, an eighth note is a quaver, a sixteenth note is a
semiquaver, and a thirty-second note is a semidemiquaver.
Americans use a moveable Do that moves according to the
position of the first note of a key. For example, Do equals E in
the key of E, or Do equals F in the key of F, and so on. The
French and others use a system called a fixed Do, in which Do
is always C. The end result is the same but if someone is
working with people from other countries it is useful to
understand their terms. In the Congo Jackie would have to use

the European system in the music classes, so it was good that she was prepared.

The French class lasted until noon and then after two hours for lunch we would meet at the school and spend the afternoon on some sort of excursion. It was a wonderful experience. The guides took us almost everywhere and showed us many places and institutions. By the end of the year we knew more about Belgium than did most of the inhabitants. We visited all types of schools, hospitals, public buildings, city halls, museums, and the *palais de justice,* which must be one of the most impressive buildings in Europe because of the size of its cavernous central hall.

The schools were among the most interesting places we visited. Unlike the United States, where almost everyone gets the same education (or lack of it), the Belgian system was more realistic. They recognized that not all individuals have the same interests and abilities. Children were tested at the sixth grade and again at the ninth grade and efforts were made to guide them to the kind of training or education they could benefit from. Those who were planning to attend a university or a similar institution were sent to a *lycée* for a thorough and demanding academic education. There were two examinations a student in a lycée had to pass, called the first and second baccalaureate, to be eligible to enroll in an institution of higher learning. There were no remedial classes at that level and no athletic scholarships. A student who was eligible to enter a university was considered to have an education equivalent to that of an American student with two years of college. The others were sent to vocational or professional schools where they would acquire the skills needed to make a living. Some of those schools included courses normally taught in American universities, such as hotel and restaurant management.

American educators generally criticize the system, saying it condemns a student in a technical school to an inferior status in society as a mechanic or a waiter and deprives him of an opportunity to improve himself. That is not true; even in the vocational schools academic subjects were not neglected and there were provisions for a late bloomer who decided that he would like to go to the university to take an examination that would make him eligible if he passed it. The system may have had some flaws, but it would have been hard to find anyone in Belgium with a valid diploma of any kind who was unable to read and write.

The same system was used all over Europe and in the United Kingdom. We visited a variety of schools; one trained students for a career in the food service and hotel industry; another was turning out skilled craftsmen in carpentry, cabinetry, and woodworking; and another specialized in metalworking. One of the remarkable features of those schools was the total absence of power tools. Those must have been introduced later, after the students had mastered the fundamentals. At the art school, students were making color separations for color lithographs by hand, a process I had heard about but had never seen. It could be said that some of the schools were not on the cutting edge of technology, but the technicians were being well trained.

Brussels was not one city but a collection of what were called communes, each with its own administration with a *bourgemestre* or mayor, its own city council, and other local government officials. It was similar to the situation in this country where some suburbs are as large as the core city.

One day we went to the commune of Scharbeek so that we could see how the government of a commune worked. We were cordially received in a large room with exquisite carved wood paneling in a building that must have been hundreds of years old. One of the city officials told us about the organization of the commune and how it functioned, and his explanation was very interesting and informative. As he talked I happened to glance into the next room and was both horrified and amused to see that some of the functionaries were pouring white wine into goblets, enough for the entire group.

What happened next was going to be interesting, because while the missionaries had serious disagreements on theological concerns there was one matter upon which most of them agreed wholeheartedly, and that was that consuming alcohol in any form was the most wicked thing anyone could do. The courteous and civilized act would have been to accept the wine and not create an unpleasant situation. If I had seen what our hosts were about to do soon enough I suppose I could have explained to them what sort of people they were dealing with and that serving wine, no matter how excellent, would not be appropriate, but it was too late.

So I assumed the role of a disinterested spectator, pretending I was not even there when the official presentation was concluded and the waiters came in with trays of fine wine while our host boasted of its quality. Our leader, Bertie, had to explain that he was sorry but that none of us drank wine. It was an embarrassing moment for a few of us, and I felt it was boorish, but I am sure that most of the others were unaware that their actions were anything but the most noble.

From there we went to the planning office where accurate and detailed records on each piece of property in the commune were kept, then on to visit a hospital and other local institutions.

We had to have a piano for Jackie, so soon after we were settled we went down to a store in a dilapidated part of the city that had an ample stock of used pianos. We arranged for the rental of a small upright piano, and it was delivered by two men, one very large and robust and the other much smaller. Just like in a 1920s motion picture comedy, the larger fellow set the piano on the back of his partner, who then carried it two flights of stairs single-handedly. (When I use the term *dilapidated,* I simply mean old and a little shabby compared to other parts of the city. Nowhere in Brussels did we see litter or signs of neglect such as we have in most American cities.)

One morning I got up as usual and prepared to go to school. As I came downstairs, got my bicycle from the back of the downstairs hall, and headed for the door, Mademoiselle came out and told me that I would not be going to school. I asked why and she replied, *"Verglas."* That was a new word for me, but I thought that if she was referring to the weather—for it was a more than usually gray, dismal day—it meant nothing to someone who had endured not only many Colorado winters but two in South Dakota and one in Connecticut. As often happened, I was wrong, because *verglas* was something I not only had never encountered but could not imagine. When I got out on the sidewalk, I found it was one solid sheet of ice, as were all the streets in the city. In Brussels the temperature rarely drops below freezing, but when it does the consequences are severe. It had rained during the night as usual and then the wet streets had frozen, covering everything with a thin but very slick coating of what is called black ice.

While the winter was rather unpleasant, spring and autumn were beautiful and we went go on picnics in Woluwe Park, about a mile or two down the bicycle path, or to Tervueren. We all had bicycles and the paths made cycling safe. The place we enjoyed going to most was Tervueren, a village near Brussels. The Congo Museum, with its impressive collection of Congo sculpture, was in a beautiful neoclassical building there. Behind the museum there were formal gardens and a fountain that were designed to resemble the palace at Versailles built by Louis XIV, though on a smaller scale. Beyond the fountain steps led down to more gardens and lawns that descended into the distance and appeared to go on forever, as at Versailles. On each side were forests that reminded us of the trees in paintings by Watteau, Boucher, and Fragonard. There were never many people there so it was a perfect setting for a picnic, and there was a little café where we could get something to drink and enjoy the beauty and tranquillity of the park.

During the first nine months we met with tutors several times a week and I also enrolled in evening classes that were free of charge and were part of what we would call an adult education program. Most of the students were from Eastern Europe and had been fortunate enough to emigrate to Belgium, but the classes were open to everyone. I still have my diploma with a grade of *très bien*. Since Jackie was not taking the French course at the Colonial School, she had a tutor during the day when the boys were in school. She was also able to get a lot of practice while shopping and with Marie, our part-time maid, and usually understood what people said better than I did. During her conversations with Marie she managed to incorporate into her otherwise fluent and proper French a number of colloquial expressions that were later a source of amusement for the Belgians we knew in the Congo.

The French course was followed by what was called the colonial course, consisting of two weeks of lectures in early August. We could hardly be expected to master all the material in nineteen courses, including the history and geography of the Congo, colonial hygiene, primitive institutions, history of Belgium, principles of colonization, and several others in just two weeks, so we started preparing for the examinations in January with tutors. We had all the lectures from the previous year that had been recorded by hand, mimeographed, and sold to the students for a modest sum. We also had history books and other information that we needed. It was really a very efficient system in that it imposed the burden of responsibility on the student, the one who has to do the learning.

The professors did not waste their time imparting information in lectures that we could acquire by reading, and they were free to spend their time in more productive pursuits. It has always seemed to me absurd that in some universities a professor will read his lectures to an assembly of several hundred students when most of them, presumably, are capable of reading the material for themselves. During my college years I was fortunate to never have attended such courses.

The examination system was also quite different from what we had known in the United States. There were no true-false or multiple-choice questions. All the examinations were oral and the professor usually asked only one question of each student, but there may have been more for some students. The students were called in individually to be examined and were alone with the examiner so there was no possibility of cheating, and the professor could tell whether the student was serious or not. If the student answered the question successfully he passed and if not, he failed. There were not many failures because we all knew how the system worked and were highly motivated to succeed.

The French professor evidently had a clear idea of who was going to pass and who was not, and for me at least, the French exam was easy. He asked the question, and I answered it. Besides, I had worked very hard and we had avoided as much as possible spending time with other Americans. It is not that we had anything against Americans, but we had better things to do than sit around and complain about Belgium, as expatriates are apt to do. We were probably considered antisocial by some of our colleagues because we did not seek them out, but we felt that we were being paid to learn French and adapt to the culture of the country where we were going to be working, so that is what we were doing. We have seen Americans and others who can work in a foreign country without actually "living" there. They never leave home and have an appalling lack of curiosity, which we could never understand because we believed one of the advantages of travel is the opportunity to have new experiences.

For the colonial course the examinations were more difficult. In the Belgian history course I was asked to name all the
rulers of Belgium since 52 B.C. In response I rattled off the
names of all the kings and emperors from Julius Caesar to King
Baudoin, the reigning monarch, with their dates. In the
examination for the Congo geography course, the fellow before
me was asked to describe the geological formations of the
Congo, a question I would have had trouble with, but when
the professor got to me he asked me to name all the main
rivers. The rivers I could handle, so there was an element of
luck in the process. The professor who had lectured very
briefly on anthropology had not been there the year before and
asked a question about something that he had not covered in
the lecture, nor was it mentioned in the printed material we
had. Knowing that he was associated with the anthropologists
at Tervueren, I managed to divert the conversation to the
Congo Museum and some of our mutual friends there.
Fortunately, I passed.

One important subject was colonization, taught by the
minister of colonies himself. The Belgians had studied the
colonial policies of the imperialist powers—Britain, France,
Portugal, and Spain—and had formulated what they hoped
would be the most rational and most successful approach of all.
One idea they came up with was that, assuming the colonies
would some day be independent, it would be better to provide
at least an elementary education for as many people as possible,
rather than send a small minority to universities as the French
and the British had done. Education of any kind was not
considered important in the Portuguese colonies. The Belgian
policy of providing education was the reason for subsidizing
primary schools even on Protestant mission stations.

They believed that if the masses were educated there
would be less chance that an educated élite would take over
and oppress the people. The theory seemed sound at the time.

They also assumed, as did everyone else in Europe and Africa, that independence was decades away and they would have time to gradually develop the educational system through secondary education and even into university. Unfortunately, there was not enough time to complete the plan, and what happened after independence was disappointing. The minister asked me to define colonialism and I recited the official definition, which seemed to me to be quite good. The minister then asked me if I thought compulsory education would be a good thing for the Congo. I replied that I did not think it would be possible, given the size of the country and the resources available. He seemed to agree and I had the feeling, during our short conversation, that he took his responsibility very seriously and that the welfare of the Congolese people was very important to him.

The people of Belgium had acquired the colonies, which included Ruanda and Urundi, by accident and were not interested in building empires as the British, French, and Portuguese had done. They inherited the Congo from King Léopold, who had assumed control of the Congo after the Berlin Conference of 1885, during which Africa was divided up among the European powers. His domain, known as the Congo Free State, was best known for the atrocities committed by some of his agents in an attempt to make the colony profitable. When he died in 1907, Belgium inherited the colony and did everything possible to atone for Léopold's sins. They pacified the country; built roads, schools, and hospitals; wiped out the slave trade; and provided an honest and efficient administration. Thus they created a climate for development of the country's resources, considered to be among the richest on the continent.

Having passed all the examinations, I received a certificate allowing me to teach in the second cycle, grades nine through twelve, of a secondary school for natives. We then had several weeks to go sightseeing and visit some of the interesting places in Belgium. During the spring break we had been to Paris, because according to a song, Paris was a great place to be in April. We could not afford to stay in a hotel in Paris, so we made an arrangement whereby we exchanged apartments with a couple who were studying there and thought it would be interesting to visit Brussels. It worked out very well and we saw again the friends with whom we had shared accommodations in New Haven. During the three hour-train trip we noticed that Hari seemed to be doing poorly with swollen cheeks and a slight fever. It was sad, but he had the mumps and spent the whole vacation in Paris in bed, so our sightseeing was limited. We took long walks, visited the Louvre, the Trocadero, the Eiffel Tower, the Champs Elysées, and other interesting places in spite of the very chilly weather.

One morning I went down to the nearby market to buy some rolls for breakfast. I told the lady I would like some *couques*. She did not understand so I pointed to some and said that was what I wanted. She informed me that those were *brioches* and made me feel as though I had done something terribly wrong. I had been speaking Belgian! In Brussels a breakfast roll was called a couque because that is the way the French would spell *koek*, the Flemish word for roll, related to the English word *cookie*. The French seemed to feel superior to the Belgians and often make them the butt of jokes, which is not very kind. The only discernible difference between Paris and Brussels, as far as I could see, was that Brussels was much cleaner and did not have a subway. The French did not sweep and wash the sidewalks every morning but the Paris subway, the Metro, was easy to use and went almost everywhere.

In August we had some friends take care of the boys while we went to Dinant, a picturesque little city on the Meuse in the Ardennes. It reminded us of home in Colorado because of the pine-covered mountains. The view from the citadel on a high ridge across the city was spectacular with the river, the bridges, and the old architecture. Fine handmade brass and copperware are made in Dinant, and we bought a fine teakettle that lasted for years. We also went to Antwerp one day on the train to see the home of Peter Paul Rubens, the great painter and diplomat. Jackie took a bus trip through the tulip fields of Holland one day, and we also visited a castle that was being restored. There were so many things of interest to see in Belgium, but we did not have the means to see all of them. Looking back, it was a wonderful experience, and if the purpose of our spending a year was to leave a positive impression of the country and the people of Belgium, the program succeeded in our case.

CHAPTER 6

*We leave Brussels, take the train to Antwerp, and board
the 'Elisabethville' for the voyage to the Congo. A very
pleasant trip. We spend a few days in Léopoldville then
go on to Lodja for language training.*

TOWARD THE END OF AUGUST, having satisfied the twelve-
month residence requirement, we packed up our belongings,
including all four bicycles, arranged for the shipment of all our
household effects, said *au revoir* to Madame and Mademoiselle
and took a train to Antwerp. There we boarded the *Elisabethville,* a beautiful one-class ship that had all the amenities of a
luxury cruise ship like the ones we now see on television,
except that there was no casino, no floor show, and no cruise
director. There was a swimming pool, and compared to the
Edam our accommodations were luxurious. Since we had
children we were given a very comfortable cabin with a private
bathroom on one of the upper decks. Some of our childless
friends who probably paid as much as we had were in a smaller
cabin on a lower deck. The Belgians were very family-oriented.

The food was fabulous. I do not think we have ever eaten
as well as that at any time in our lives. We could have anything
we wanted, and it was all superbly prepared. The waiters took a
genuine interest in the boys and gave them a lot of special
attention, which we thought was very kind. If the boys
declined to eat something the waiter would tell them it was
lion or crocodile or something equally exotic. Then they
tended to cooperate.

The voyage to Matadi, the main port of the Congo, by way
of Lobito Bay in Angola took two glorious weeks. On the way

we stopped at Tenerife in the Canary Islands. It was a beautiful place with lush, green hills behind the port, but the people appeared to be quite poor. We visited the local handicrafts shops and some of our friends who were more skilled at tourism than we were told us that we would be making a big mistake if we did not buy what they called Madeira lace. We bought an embroidered tablecloth after protracted haggling and were convinced we had outsmarted the peddler. Later we saw the same thing in the Montgomery Ward catalog for the same price or less.

Most of the passengers were Belgians, either colonial administrators or employees of the mining and other industries that were the main source of colonial wealth, but there were also quite a few missionaries on board. One middle-aged woman was from our mission and stayed pretty close to us much of the time. We asked her many questions and learned much about what to expect during the time we spent with her. We usually had dinner at the same table and one evening we were served baked Alaska for dessert. The waiter brought it out with great ceremony on a little cart, poured brandy over it and lit it to cook the meringue. She refused to eat it because the brandy was alcohol, even though the waiter assured her that all the alcohol had been consumed in the flames. Baked Alaska is something we do not see every day so we went ahead and ate it, not caring what she thought. She was taking with her a case of bottles of a tonic for the girls entrusted to her care. We were amused when she later discovered that the tonic contained fifteen percent alcohol, like some of the tonics that were so popular in the South during prohibition.

One evening apple pie was served for dessert and we casually mentioned to the waiter that Americans usually served a little cheese with their apple pie. He found that strange, but being well trained to please he went back to the kitchen and returned with a huge tray with a dozen different kinds of cheese on it, slightly overdoing it. To him that was normal because Europeans often serve a selection of cheeses before or after the dessert course of a proper dinner. I do not remember which it is and the order may vary from country to country.

The boys and I usually swam every day but I still had a lot of time on my hands so I started doing sketches and cartoons of the people on the ship. I also had some watercolor paper so I finished some of the cartoons in watercolor. I was only doing them for myself but the purser saw them and found them particularly amusing because they depicted things that had happened on board the ship. During a gala that was held one evening he auctioned them off to the passengers. We split the proceeds with half going to some charity and the other half to me, my share being about fifty dollars. Our missionary friend was displeased, but I did not think it was any of her business.

Something that made the voyage exciting was crossing the equator. On the day we crossed there was an elaborate ceremony with Neptune in all his regalia, surrounded by a host of appropriately-costumed attendants, holding court. Many of the passengers were painted up, some were required to pay a fine or receive some sort of punishment and most us had to crawl through a large canvas tube while being soaked with water from a fire hose. Everyone seemed to be having a great time and we all have certificates saying that we have received the baptism of the equator.

During the voyage the personnel of the ship had been very attentive and had given us excellent service, but as soon a we arrived in Matadi all that changed. Jackie and Paul immediately took a plane to Léopoldville but Hari and I had to stay in Matadi until the next day, which meant that we had to spend the night on the ship before we could proceed by land. I was a little disappointed that the stewards acted as though they had never seen us before, probably because we had not been able to tip as generously as most of the other passengers whose income was much greater than ours. Food service ceased but we were allowed to stay in a small cabin without air-conditioning but filled with hungry mosquitoes. I remember one of the stewards in particular. He was wearing shorts and his skin was a pale, sickly white which seemed out of place in the tropics. That was understandable because on the ship he worked from early morning until late at night and had no time for sunbathing. On board the ship he was responsible for maintaining several cabins, making the beds and cleaning and also had to work in the dining room at every meal. I have never seen people work as hard as those stewards did. I asked him how he was and he replied, "*Ca roule comme une boîte carrée dans le sable,*" which means "It rolls like a square box in the sand," a rather picturesque expression that might mean things are not going well.

In the morning we got up early and went to the customs shed where our baggage was. We were early because we wanted to get an early start, and we had to not only clear through customs our own belongings, including several trunks, but also had to clear the car we had agreed to drive to Léopoldville, more than 150 miles away, because the owner had been held up somewhere and could not be there to drive it himself. We had no idea what the road was like but we soon found out. It was rough going and we were told that the road was purposely poorly maintained so that travelers would be encouraged to take the train instead of driving.

A customs official came and began going through our baggage. He had me open every trunk and suitcase and went through everything with painful deliberation, examining every book to make sure there was nothing subversive, I suppose. My impatience must have irritated him because he kept addressing me as *tu*, the familiar form, instead of *vous*, the polite form. When he finally finished he told me I had to pay five dollars duty on the perfume. Missionaries were supposed to be allowed entry duty free, except for a ten percent duty on

This is how we looked boarding the 'Elisabethville'. The package under my arm was a blanket we had forgotten to pack.

The first thing we did in Léopoldville was to buy the regulation pith helmets to protect us from the tropical sun.

automobiles, so I was about to protest, saying I had no perfume, but I realized the five dollars was really for my impatience and lack of respect for the functionary. Ever since, I have always been very courteous and submissive when going through customs.

I paid the five dollars, picked up the car, and we were on our way. Our baggage went by train to Léopoldville and then up the Congo River and the Sankuru to Lusambo where it would be picked up by the mission truck and taken to Wembo Nyama, our final destination. The car we were driving was a Chevrolet Carryall that belonged to the engineer who was coming out to oversee the building of a hospital at Wembo Nyama. He had thought he was buying a truck or at least a heavy-duty vehicle, but it had essentially the same chassis and suspension system as a sedan. It was loaded with tools, quite overloaded actually, so we drove all the way to Luluabourg, about 750 miles in all, with the springs flattened out and the chassis bumping on the axle. It was better suited for trips to the grocery store than driving on barely-discernible unpaved roads.

We arrived in Léopoldville and found it to be a beautiful city with wide tree-lined boulevards, shops, restaurants, and gracious residential areas. We stayed for several days at the Union Mission House, a sort of hotel run by and for missionaries. Jackie and Paul were already there and it was good to get back together. We had to register at the American consulate, a small office in a shabby ochre-colored building. After we had completed the formalities the woman who waited on us said, "If you get into any trouble out there don't expect any help from us." The city was named for King Léopold by his agent, Henry Morton Stanley, who felt such a designation was more appropriate than the name of the village, Kinshasa, that was already there. After independence the name was changed to Kinshasa.

I thought we should let the folks back home know that we

had arrived safely, so I wrote some letters and went to the post office to mail them. There was a long line, all Africans, so I got in line and was ready to wait my turn. I was then told by the men in front of me to go to the head of the line. I was reluctant but they urged me to do so and one of them told me that there were very few white people in the country and those were there were engaged in some essential occupation and did not have time to stand in line. I had not thought about it, but the immigration policy was very restrictive and residence visas were only given to those who could be of service in some way.

One of the things I remember about the Union Mission House is the two South African men staying there. They were very pious and spoke and acted like real missionaries, only more so, and I could not help feeling that there was something about them that did not ring quite true. One of them was a very skilled artist who did beautiful watercolor and gouache paintings that he was trying to sell to finance their mission. They were involved in what seemed to be a very implausible project. They said their mission was to travel throughout the world, working with nurses and encouraging then to become born-again Christians. They spoke the right jargon, they had the right mannerisms, and seemed to have fooled everyone except me. I could not help having reservations about them and thought of what a good cover religion could be for some-one who wants to take advantage of others.

Léopoldville was located at what was called Stanley Pool, a place where the Congo River widens out before beginning a long, gradual descent through rapids that eliminate any possi-bility of ocean-going vessels ever making use of the extensive internal river system. Over a distance of 150 miles the river descends about 1,000 feet. The cataracts, as they are called, constitute one of the most perfect sites in the world for hydroelectric power. Some power plants have now been built, but the potential remains for much more when the country has an honest and stable government and is developed sufficiently so that there is a market for the product. The middle of the country is a large basin ranging from 1,000 to 1,500 feet above sea level, with rain forest in the far northern part of the country changing to mixed forest and savannah and finally savannah and grassland in the far south. The Congo River starts as the Lualaba near Lake Tanganyika, flows north across the equator, then west and finally south so that at any time half the river and its tributaries are in a region that is having its rainy season. Consequently, the flow of the Congo is very stable and does not vary much with the seasons. The Congo and its many navigable tributaries are the principal means of transportation, augmented by a few roads and railroads. On the river there were very comfortable Mississippi-type river boats and we were looking forward to a leisurely trip up the river that had been described as the experience of a lifetime. It may have been, because now it is not possible.

Because we had agreed to drive our friend's Carryall we were not able to take the river boat, but looking back on it now, the trip by road was also an experience to be remembered, because it was also something that would be nearly impossible to do now. Even if the roads are passable there is a problem of security that did not exist then. Jackie and Paul went on to Luluabourg by plane while Hari and I drove. We left on Monday and even though it was probably only 750 miles we finally arrived in Luluabourg on Saturday. The first night we stayed in a hotel but after that we stopped at mission stations because there were no hotels for several hundred miles. We were always welcome, as were all travelers in that undeveloped part of the Congo, and we were well taken care of. The roads were only one lane and mostly either rough or in deep sand or mud so going was slow, and if we met another car one of us was courteous and got out of the way. Even that did not happen often because traffic was very light.

The first mission station we stopped at, a station of the Baptist Foreign Missions Society, was at Boko, about forty miles beyond Popokabaka. We arrived after dark after traveling since six o'clock in the morning, so we were very tired and glad to be there.

In the guest house were two beautiful ceremonial masks of the Bayaka tribe. It was interesting that the missionaries did not seem to be interfering with the traditional customs of the inhabitants. The boys of the tribe who had just reached puberty had just completed their initiation ceremony, during which they had probably been circumcised and had been taught secrets limited to adults and had participated in rituals that were necessary for them to become male members of the tribe. It was the custom for each boy to make the mask he would use in the ceremony and discard after the initiation. I asked if I could have one of the masks, so the missionary sold it to me for twenty francs, which she would give to the boy who made it. The next morning we just put it in the car on top of everything else and took off on our journey, not thinking about the mask in the back seat. From then on every time we stopped we would have a crowd around the car talking excitedly and gesticulating. Then one of them would ask to see the mask. I always handed it over to whomever asked for it because I felt that he was just curious and would not harm the mask. After an interested inspection of the interior he would put it over his head and begin to dance for the entertainment of his friends. Another even ran down to his village some half mile away to show it to his neighbors and relatives. Each tribe has its own masks, done in a style unique to that tribe and it is doubtful that most of them had ever seen a mask from another tribe. That must account for the great interest our Bayaka mask aroused. At a river where some friends who were also driving into the interior had just boarded a ferry, ready to cross the river, the crew deserted the ferry and came to look at the mask, leaving our friends sitting and waiting. We finally hid the mask because it was attracting too much attention and we were afraid it would be worn out before we reached our destination.

I mentioned the ferries. Between Matadi and Léopoldville there were bridges over the rivers because they were small and the bridges were strange. They were one-way bridges and so narrow that grooves were worn in the sides by the hubs of the trucks. But from Léopoldville on there were no bridges. Instead there were ferries and some of the rivers like the Kwango and the Kwilu were as wide as the Mississippi.

There were several types of ferries. Some had an engine and were built like ferries in Europe, with a steel hull and a large deck area; some were attached to a cable and were propelled across the river by the current, but those were limited to the smaller rivers. The most interesting were those like the one on which we crossed the Louange and several other rivers. It consisted of several dugout canoes with two-inch thick planks laid across them, the whole thing lashed together with vines. The ferry was commanded by a *kapita,* Congolese for captain or anyone in charge of something. He was quite elderly and extremely dignified. He was wearing an old American army campaign hat with a gold button on the front, a military coat, and a piece of cloth wrapped around his waist.

When we arrived at the ferry at nine o'clock in the morning there was another car that had been waiting for half an hour for the crew to show up—an example of the meaninglessness of time in Africa. The men in the village simply had not yet made up their minds to come down to the river and begin their day's work so we had to wait until they did. They took the car that had been waiting and then came back for us. By that time another car had arrived so they put both cars on at the same time. The crew of about a dozen men, with teeth filed to a point that gave them a terrifying appearance, poled the ferry along the bank to a predetermined spot upstream. They then exchanged their poles for paddles and rowed us across. They had calculated everything exactly right and we arrived on the other side at the landing.

We then had to cross a mudflat for about twenty feet and then climb a steep bank to reach the road. That no one else had gotten stuck encouraged us and we went up the bank and onto the road. The crossing had taken about an hour because of the time it took to pole up the river but it was fun and we were on our way to Mukedi, the next mission station on our itinerary.

Mukedi was a beautiful place with nice modern homes, electricity that was out of order and several people we had known in Brussels. We enjoyed a fine dinner with old friends, a dinner that included mango sauce, applesauce made with mangoes instead of apples. It was our introduction to the way we would try to duplicate familiar things with what was available locally. For example, unripe plantains were a good substitute for potato chips when thinly sliced and fried in deep fat.

The next morning we set out for Kikwit. There the mission had been receiving so many visitors that it had been turned into an inn, which must have distracted it from its main purpose, but it had no choice because there was no place else for travelers to stay for more than 100 miles.

When we asked for directions to a mission we discovered that when a Congolese said "mission" he meant a Protestant mission. He referred to the Catholic mission as "Mon Père," from the French form of addressing a priest, which he pronounced *mon pèlè.* Most Congolese had trouble with the letter *r* and generally ended each word with a vowel. As we approached Luluabourg we crossed the Lulua River on a large ferry with an engine. The ferry was crowded with people from the area who were going to the city. As I looked out of the window of the car I saw a woman squatting on the deck eating live flying ants soaked in palm oil from a coffee can. The ants were considered a delicacy and when they swarm everyone wanted to catch as many as possible.

We arrived in Luluabourg after only a few minor difficulties like having the windshield wipers quit during a violent downpour. While not as grand as Léopoldville, Luluabourg was a fine looking city, named after the local tribe, with some paved streets, a hotel, movie theater, ice cream parlor, and a general store. It was on the rail line that ran from Port Franqui on the Kasai River to Elisabethville in the Katanga and then on to South Africa. For us it was a very welcome sight after such a long trip through country almost entirely devoid of the amenities of civilization. We had to stay at the hotel near the airport for several days to await the arrival of the owner of the Carryall to pick it up. On Sunday we visited the Presbyterian mission and found the people to be very hospitable.

We were driven to Lodja, where we were to spend six months in language training, in a Chevrolet station wagon by one of our colleagues who had come to pick us up. It was a two-day trip, so we planned to spend the night at a British mission station about half way. It was in a dense, dark, and gloomy forest and when we arrived well after the sun had gone down a heavy rain added to the dismal atmosphere. We had been delayed several hours because we had to wait until a large tree that had fallen across the road was removed by several men with small axes. We were met by a dwarf carrying a kerosene lantern who guided us into the house.

Our hosts greeted us warmly and proudly showed us the new upright piano that had just arrived from England for their daughter. It must have taken them a long time to save up enough for such a luxury and it obviously meant a great deal to them to have for their daughter to have an instrument to play. The next morning the sun was shining and the rain had stopped so everything had a more cheerful aspect than it had the night before.

It was becoming difficult to find any place that was not affected by the march of civilization, and some of the imported products were neither necessary not desirable.

The natives were always too polite to tell us when we had made a mistake, but I am sure we provided a lot of entertainment when we spoke Otetela.

We continued our journey northward and after crossing the Lukenie River on a cable ferry we went east through fairly open country on the edge of the forest to Lodja, where we were to complete an intensive course in Otetela, the local language. On the way to Lodja we passed through an area inhabited by what were called the Bankutu or Basongo-Meno, who had been known in the early days as cannibals and fiercely inhospitable. They lived in the dense forest and were difficult to subdue because with their bows and poisoned arrows they had a military advantage over government troops with rifles on the narrow jungle paths. In an effort to make peace with them the administrator sent them a gift of two rifles, carried by messengers. Several days later a member of the tribe returned the rifles, saying they did not want them but they would welcome more messengers. They had eaten them. However, when we were there they had become peaceful and cooperative with the government.

Lodja was an important administrative center boasting a government hospital, a filling station, and a butcher shop that sold fresh beef from cattle brought up from the Katanga by truck. That was a rare luxury because the tsetse fly that causes sleeping sickness in both humans and animals made it impossible to raise cattle in the central Congo. The fly did not seem to affect sheep, goats, or wild animals. This was the only butcher ship in the entire Sankuru District and our only source of beef for the next four years. If someone went to Lodja from Wembo Nyama he would take along an insulated box and bring back some beef packed in ice for everyone, but that did not happen often. Recreational driving was rare and most people only traveled when necessary.

At Lodja a new mud house with a thatched roof had been built for us and we found it quite cool and comfortable. There were screens on the windows and the ceiling was covered with hand-woven mats like the ones that covered most of the dirt floor. The walls were whitewashed with a mixture of kaolin and manioc paste that still had a sour odor, having been done very recently. It was all very fresh and clean and the only problem was getting used to the snakes and spiders in the roof who had moved in even before we did. We all had mosquito nets that we were very careful to tuck in properly every night to protect us from the mosquitoes. We also learned to take our anti-malarial drugs regularly and to always wear our white pith helmets any time we went outside. We were learning how to adapt to life four degrees south of the equator. We had electricity for four hours every evening as long as the generator was working, but we always kept our Coleman lamps in case of a power outage. The generator was made in Britain and chugged along at 600 to 800 revolutions per minute and required less maintenance than American machines that ran at a much higher speed.

Our six months at Lodja were to be devoted exclusively to the study of Otetela, so that by the time we actually started working we would be able to communicate satisfactorily. The course was taught by a very serious young man who spoke French very well and was an excellent teacher, incorporating some of the best principles of language instruction. In the class there was also a young Belgian who had arrived about the same time and was there to teach agriculture in the monitors school. He had done his *stage* or practical training in the vineyards in France and knew more about raising grapes than anything else, but he did have a good solid education in all aspects of agriculture. Even though his specialty was of little use because the soil and the climate were not suitable for grapes, there were still many things he could do to improve the agricultural practices of the area. The main problem he faced, and one which people who have not lived there cannot understand, is that Africans tend to be very conservative and do not embrace new ideas readily.

Our teacher used many pattern sentences, such as, "I put the bricks in the box. They put the bricks in the box," and so on. To liven up the class a little and relieve the tedium of endless repetition—repetition essential in successful language learning—we began to be creative and invent sentences that were pure nonsense. For example we would say, "We put the bricks in the bottle." The teacher would shake his head and say, "You cannot put the bricks in the bottle." It made no differences as far as the syntax was concerned because the purpose was to learn the structure of the language, but the teacher had a very literal mind and anything that was not logical bothered him. Naturally, we stopped doing it. Although I have forgotten much of the Otetela I had learned, I can still remember that *atafadi* meant bricks and *elondo* meant bottles.

People in industrialized countries tend to believe that languages in primitive societies are rudimentary and uncomplicated. Otetela was neither. If anything, the grammar and syntax were quite the opposite. English, for example, is both simpler and less logical. While French has two genders and German three, Otetela has six categories, each forming the plural in a different way. The language is also to some extent tonal, meaning that if the voice goes up a word means one thing, if it remains level it means another and if it goes down it means something else. The example given to illustrate the tones was *Kónde, konde, kònde*, which means The alligator does not eat beans. The first word has a high tone, the second a middle tone and the third a low tone. You can imagine how amusing it could be when a foreigner uses the wrong tone and says something nonsensical.

Sometimes the length of a vowel is phonemic. If the vowel is short it means one thing and if it is dragged out it means something else. The verb tenses in Otetela are very precise, with one tense for something that happened today and another for something that happened before today. It is also an agglutinating language so that the verb root or infinitive, the tense indicator and pronouns are all one word with only a letter or group of letters to represent each one. It is also a very pleasant language to listen to.

Some of the missionaries spoke the language fluently but others whose hearing was not as acute did not pronounce everything exactly right and the Africans were too polite to call attention to their errors. There had developed over the years a dialect understood on and near the mission station but not in the outlying villages. We had a demonstration of that while we were in Lodja. We went to church two or three times on Sunday and several times went out to villages some distance from Lodja with the district superintendent. He was a fiery preacher and his Otetela was impressive.

He would stand up and preach to the congregation for almost an hour in a little thatch-roofed church when the temperature was over ninety degrees and the humidity about the same. I admired the patience of the crowd. The congregation would then drone through a few hymns that had been translated into Otetela, but using the original American or English music. The music being as foreign to them as the English words would have been, they sounded as though they were singing in a foreign language without understanding the words. After the hymns and some lengthy prayers, Papa Gandjolo, an elderly African preacher would get up and talk for half an hour or so. Curious, I asked him one day why he preached after the district superintendent had finished and he replied, "The district superintendent speaks Otetela so badly that the people did not have any idea of what he was trying to say, so I told them what he said."

We were in Lodja for Christmas and somehow it did not seem like Christmas at all. In Belgium we had put out wooden shoes instead of hanging up stockings for Christmas and followed other Belgian customs but it still seemed like Christmas. The presents sent by the grandparents had not arrived so we had to dispense with the usual ritual of having lots of things under the tree to guess about and the suspense that goes with opening everything. The boys did get some crayons and some soccer balls but that was all until the Christmas party in town. I got a fountain pen and Jackie received a demitasse cup to add to her small collection and a handbag I had bought in Léopoldville from one of the traders from the north. For a Christmas tree we had some palm branches tied together with ornaments hanging from them. It was Hari's invention and we were proud of the way he put the tree up and took it down. Someone told us that Christmas lasted from November until Easter and we could see what she meant.

We had several parties during the Christmas season. Christmas Eve we went to the Wamamas' (the single ladies' residence) for dessert with limeade, cookies, nuts, and other delicacies. In Otetela *mama* is the word for madam, Miss, or Mrs., and the plural is *Wamama*. There we sang Christmas carols and opened the presents we had for each other. On Christmas day we had a big dinner with a pork roast—a real treat, potatoes, sweet potatoes, beans, and a pineapple and banana salad, then ice cream and fruitcake for dessert. It may seem strange to consider potatoes a delicacy but they do not grow well in hot climates and have to be imported, and anything that has to be imported takes on special value.

We noticed that although there was a sizable expatriate community in Lodja and a *Cercle* or social club, the missionaries did not take part in any of the social activities because of cultural differences. The annual Christmas party seemed to be one of the few events were fraternization was permitted or unavoidable so we went. We were cordially received by the District Administrator who had us seated and ordered lemonade for us. We sat and talked with various people and then the children went up to receive their gifts from *Père Noël*, each one receiving a jar of candy, a box of colored pencils, and a coloring book.

The next evening we had the rest of the pork, which had come from the local butcher shop. Although a few pigs were raised on a casual basis by the local people, and there were wild pigs, we hesitated to use them because they were liable to be filled with parasites. Besides, processing pork into ham, bacon, pork roasts, and so on required a skill and art generally unavailable among the indigenous population.

Having come from a dry climate we were unprepared to deal with such things as mold and mildew. In Lodja everything is affected by mildew unless one is constantly vigilant. Leather is particularly susceptible and it was not uncommon to take shoes out of the closet and find them covered with a uniform coating that looked like green velvet, both inside and out. The solution was to take our clothes out and hang them in the sun periodically to dry them out. We had to do the same thing with books and some of them seemed to attract mildew more than others. I do not remember Tarzan having problems like that in the movies we saw.

Another thing that was new to us was termites. Encouraged by the heat and the dampness, they were constantly at work in the walls and woodwork, quietly eating away at the wooden poles in the walls and the rafters. Houses built as ours was would eventually collapse but that took years so we did not have anything to worry about in our new house.

While we were at Lodja in language training, Fernand had his meals with us. I wanted very much for the boys to keep up their French so we adopted a system whereby we one day we would put a small Belgian flag on the table and we would speak French. The next day we would put an American flag on the table and we would speak English, because Fernand was still working to perfect his English. The boys refused to cooperate. They would speak French with anyone outside the family but refused to speak it with us. They were in Africa now and French was what they spoke in Belgium. It was not long until they were communicating very well in Otetela and were forgetting French. Then when we returned to the United States they forgot Otetela as well. We were sorry to see them losing their language ability but there was nothing we could do about it. Children have a logic of their own that tells them what language they should be speaking. It was our experience that when placed with their peers in a foreign country they quickly learned the language. There might be a lesson there for those who are promoting bilingual education.

It was at Lodja that we first learned about the entrepreneurial aspect of missionary work. I had assumed, if I thought about it at all, that we all received about the same compensation, with adjustments for length of service and family size and that funding of mission projects like the school where we would be teaching would be the responsibility of the Board of Missions. I also knew that missionaries were encouraged to assist in raising funds for mission projects and that fund-raising could contribute to the success of the mission. It looked like a logical and efficient system.

Then I discovered that missionaries could solicit contributions which did not go to the Board of Missions for disbursement but to them personally. One of the missionaries at Lodja had been there for four years and was going on furlough for a year, a year that would be spent visiting as many churches as possible to raise money for the mission and for his own needs. He was going to sell his Chevrolet station wagon for nearly as much as he had paid for it, taking advantage of the strong demand for American automobiles in the Congo. He had, during the four years he had used it during his frequent trips to visit local pastors, collected enough reimbursement based on the mileage to replace it, and he had also already raised enough in contributions from churches at home for a new one.

I wondered about the practice but decided it was not my place to judge. I also knew that in most cases missionaries who were successful fund-raisers spent everything they got on some mission-related project like a village dispensary or a roof for a pastor's house. This man may have been doing the same thing, but just using an automobile as the purpose because being without one in the heart of darkest Africa was something people at home could relate to. Such an appeal would cause potential donors to open their purses and checkbooks without hesitation. I have never liked asking people for money and did not intend to participate in fund-raising because I was going to be teaching in a school and saw no need for it. Later, when Jackie did need to pay for the expense of hiring the mission truck to take the school choir on short trips to put on concerts, she relied upon donations from her home church in Denver.

We were doing quite well in our language studies, but suddenly had them cut short because the fellow who had gone out a year ahead of us had died of polio and we had to move to Wembo Nyama to begin teaching after only three months of language study. Central Congo is not one of the healthiest places on earth, with the heat and the dampness being so favorable to all sorts of insects and microbes, but what had killed Max, according to the doctor, was his paranoid fear of germs and disease. Because he had such a high standard of hygiene he did not absorb germs in small quantities as most people do. As a result had failed to build up any antibodies, so that when he was attacked by a virus it proved fatal.

Max's death was unfortunate, because everyone had been dreaming of the day when there would be enough qualified professional teachers in the *Ecole de Moniteurs*, the high school–level teacher training school. The purpose of the school was to train teachers to teach in the network of primary schools the mission maintained in the villages that, along with rural dispensaries, were part of the mission's service to the community. At that time almost all schools were organized and run by missions. Some of the missionaries taught part-time in the schools on the mission station, and there were two very good African teachers, so the monitors school got by, though just barely.

It was just a small detail that was overlooked, but no one told us that if we did not bring an automobile we would be without transportation, and when we got to Lodja we began to understand what we had gotten ourselves into. Every place we would want to go was at least 100 miles from anywhere else and there was no public transportation, so some form of transportation other than bicycles was essential. We had assumed that the mission would have some means of providing transportation when necessary, but the reality was that if someone did not have a motor car he could not go anywhere. The prospect of spending four years on a remote mission station with no means of escape was not pleasant. Fortunately, when Max's widow found out we did not have a car she passed on to us the 1952 Chevrolet sedan they had brought out the year before.

It was the custom of the people to give all foreigners working among them an African name so they would not have to struggle with names that were difficult to pronounce and remember. When we had been at Lodja long enough for them to see what we were like, they gave each of us a name that they felt expressed in some way our appearance or personality. We were told that they also had another name for each of us known only to the Congolese themselves that was more descriptive and less complimentary than the name we were given publicly. We were certainly a source of amusement to the Congolese, because of our bizarre behavior and incomprehensible ways, but they rarely, if ever, revealed their true feelings. At the same time they were very skilled at discerning ours.

For me they selected the name Fundji, so I was known as Uwandji Fundji, *Uwandji* being the Otetela equivalent of the Swahili term *Bwana,* an honorific used to address those in a position of authority. I was named after the respected chief of a village not far from Lodja and one day we went to visit the real Uwandji Fundji. He was a dignified, elderly man wearing a military tunic. There was a short ceremony during which I was given my African name and Jackie was given the name of one of his wives. Our older son was given the name Tshupa, which we were told meant Little Bottle, and Paul, since he had a biblical name, was called Paulo Tambena.

Then a few weeks later a delegation came to tell us that Jackie's name would have to be changed because the wife whose name she had been given had run off. Batetela women enjoyed considerable freedom and were by no means oppressed as women in some other societies are. If a woman felt she was being mistreated or was not pleased with her husband she could go back to her family and her father would have to refund the bride price the husband had paid. Jackie's original name, Owoyolo, was changed to Mama Uyaka, which means singer or musician. She seemed surprised and asked how I felt about the change. I told her, "At least I won't have to worry about another change as long as you keep playing the piano." By that time she had been playing the piano in church and conducting the choir, so a name reflecting her profession was most appropriate, particularly since artists and musicians were highly respected there. A wood carver, for example, always carried his adze on his shoulder as a badge of office and was exempt from any kind of manual labor.

CHAPTER 7

We finally arrive in Wembo Nyama and move into our house. The mission station and the school are described.

FINALLY, AFTER TWO YEARS of preparation we were going to reach our destination and start to work. First we went into Lodja to do some shopping, which was an all day affair because we did not feel much like hurrying in the heat and had to go to at least three stores that catered to Europeans. We bought a gallon of Coca-Cola syrup and a siphon to make our own soda, an indispensable item. Then we stocked up on Coleman lanterns, kerosene lamps, candles, washtubs of various sizes, large pots in which to boil our drinking water, a water filter, several buckets for carrying water, and a new teakettle. So they would not be left out, we also bought the boys some small buckets that we painted red.

Then there were the groceries. There were some imported canned goods but they were too expensive and we felt we could do without them. We would only be able to order supplies once a month in Wembo Nyama, so we had to get a generous supply of necessities to take with us from Lodja. We bought twelve kilos of sugar, a barrel of flour, and enough other staples to last a month. The trip to Wembo Nyama only took a day or so and it was very restful to drive through open country with grass three feet tall as far as we could see, grass that was beautiful but, except for providing the material for the thatched roofs, useless because it was not at all nutritious. The heavy rains leached out all the minerals that would normally have been present so the appearance of lush fertility was deceptive.

Wembo Nyama was on the main road from Lusambo, the river port on the Sankuru River, to Katako Kombe, the territorial headquarters. At the entrance to the station on the north side of the road stood a huge tree majestically standing alone. Flanked by roads on both sides was a well-kept lawn, like a park, that ran the length of the compound. A few large mango trees, widely spaced, provided shade. On the left side was the hospital, beyond which were five residences spaced far enough apart to allow for large vegetable gardens behind them. On the right was an imposing Romanesque-style church built of handmade brick. The doors and windows had round arches and were wide open, having neither glass nor screens. The galvanized metal roof was one of few on the mission station, because the use of metal roofing subject to rust had been banned by the government for aesthetic reasons after the church was built. Anyone who has flown over sprawling cities in West Africa such as Ibadan in Nigeria can appreciate that decision.

Beyond the church were several more residences, and at the far end of the compound was the single ladies' residence and dormitories for the girls in the boarding department of the primary school. Behind the church to the right was the monitors school with four buildings. One had five classrooms and a small office, one was devoted to arts and crafts, one served as a dining hall, and there were two dormitories for the boarding students, all boys or young men. There were also some small individual houses for the married students. The main building of the school was of the same architecture as the church but the dining hall was wide open with no walls except the pillars that held up the roof.

We moved into what was probably the oldest brick house. It had a metal roof, a large living room and dining room, two bedrooms, a study and a bathroom. The kitchen was about thirty feet behind the house, connected by a covered walkway.

The reason—which may have been a southern custom brought in by the missionaries—was that the danger of fire was much greater in the kitchen and if it did catch fire the house would be spared. Since we had no fire department it was a prudent thing to do. To cope with the ants and other crawling things the legs of the kitchen table were set in cans of water and the cupboards were suspended from the ceiling by wires and had screen doors for ventilation. I did not visit the kitchen often because the sight of the huge flying cockroaches disheartened me. One day I asked Jackie why the cook, Papa Shuku, was sifting the flour to remove little black things. She replied, "Those are just weevils that get into the flour, but he usually gets all of them. He has to do the same thing with the rice."

We kept the kerosene refrigerator in the dining room. Attached to the kitchen was the magazine, or store room where we kept groceries and other supplies. There was also a separate wash house, a simple open shed with a metal roof where the laundry was done and then pressed by hand with irons heated over a wood fire to kill parasites.

The house had concrete floors covered with mats made locally in place of the kind of rugs we were used to. All the furniture had been made in the school carpenter shop of fine hardwood from the forest, and the glassless windows had screens and curtains in the American style. Each bed had a mosquito net, which we were always careful to tuck in when we went to bed or took our siesta. The only room in the house that had glass in the windows was the study, which faced south, because occasionally the heavy rain would be accompanied by a strong south wind.

With screens on the windows and screen doors we had very few insects in the house. Europeans we met seemed to believe that screens impeded the flow of air and did not want to have them. I never have found out how they dealt with mosquitoes. We had a bathroom with rudimentary indoor plumbing, including a wash basin and bathtub made of bricks and coated with concrete. Only the toilet was imported. Water for everything but drinking came from cisterns that were filled with water from the roof during the rainy season. Usually, enough would be collected to last through the dry season, but if not someone would bring it from a spring down the hill. Drinking water came from the spring and was boiled and filtered before use.

The house had been well designed with high ceilings and large windows so that it was always comfortable. Behind the house was a large garden area and a small brick chicken house with a dilapidated chicken wire fence that would have to be repaired before we could start to raise chickens. There were plenty of challenges to provide the boys with experiences they would not have had at home. All our household effects arrived about the same time from home, and unpacking all the boxes and barrels was just like having Christmas because there were all kinds of surprises. Some of our things were in fifty-gallon steel barrels that had originally held margarine or cooking oil in bulk for industrial use. They had been thoroughly cleaned and had a lid that was held in place by a steel band with a hasp and padlock, making them quite secure. They were ideal for shipping to Africa. After we unpacked them all the barrels and boxes were put in the storeroom and the house began to look as though it belonged to us.

Before going any further, perhaps I should explain about the "boys," not our sons but the men who worked for us. I suppose the reason they were called boys was that the French referred to a male servant as a *boy,* and in some cases a female servant was called a *boyesse*. It is amusing to watch the reaction of some people at home when we explain to them casually that we managed to get by with as few as five servants, not counting the students who mowed our lawn with machetes or the night watchman. Most middle-class Americans seem to have the impression that there is something evil about having household help. However, in the area where we lived there were no gas and electric companies, no filling stations, no dry cleaners, no water boards, or any of the other services people in developed countries take for granted. In the Congo what would be called services had to be performed by individuals, so having servants was absolutely essential. Not only did we need them but we were expected to provide as much work as possible for the local people, and if we had not done so we would have been despised because they would have concluded that we did not like or trust them.

First of all, we had to have a cook so that Jackie would not have to spend all her time in the kitchen and would be free to teach her own offspring and also teach music and pedagogy in the mission schools. Then too, if we had chicken, as we often did once we got our poultry operation going, someone had to kill and dress the chicken and that was something neither of us had been trained to do. We brought Papa Shuku with us from Lodja as well as Shinga, the houseboy, and they both worked out very well. Shinga's job was to clean the house and help the cook in the kitchen.

According to local custom, and this is a practice seemingly applied wherever domestic help is accepted, each member of the domestic staff has clearly defined duties and there is a definite hierarchy respected by everyone. We had one man whose duty it was to do the laundry, washing it by hand and ironing everything. Another fellow gathered wood in the forest and chopped it into firewood. I did not even know we had hired anyone to chop wood until I got out a new machete and a new hatchet I had bought for my own use and showed them to some of the men. One of them took the tools out of my hands and thanked me for them. I later learned that he was our wood boy and he thought I had bought the tools for him, and so I had.

The wood boy's duties were very important to our well-being. Outside the bathroom were three fifty-gallon drums on a raised platform. They were there to provide water for the bathroom and one of his chores was to be sure that they were always full of water. Under one of them was a place to build a fire and he was also responsible for building a fire so that we could have a hot bath before dinner, a daily ritual that was a necessity in that climate.

The blade of the ax he used had been made from a broken car spring by a local blacksmith. The blacksmiths, using fifty-gallon drums and car springs for raw materials, did some amazing things with the most primitive tools. Although his ax could be used its small size made his work more difficult, so I ordered a fine double-bitted ax from Montgomery Ward, requesting that it be sent by air mail because our need was so urgent. The business of air freight was not as well organized then as it is today and although the shipping cost about four times as much as the ax it still took three months to get there. The ax worked very well and the wood boy was pleased to have it but he kept breaking the handle. Then I would take it over to the school carpenter and have him whittle out a new one, using wood that was at least as hard as hickory or ash. I finally told him that if he broke one more handle he was fired. With that incentive no more handles were broken.

The water from our cisterns was not considered fit for human consumption so our drinking water came from a spring along the shallow slope leading down to a small stream on the west side of the compound. Using a pole with a bucket on each end he would carry it up to the kitchen and deliver it to the cook who would boil it and then pour it into a filter that had porcelain candles to remove any impurities.

Plenty of food was available. We had rice, millet, peanuts, black-eyed peas, manioc, sweet potatoes, corn, palm nuts, and of course various citrus fruits, bananas, papayas, mangoes, and pineapples. We also had a breadfruit tree that shaded the back yard but the fruit we did not care for. Some things, like lettuce, tomatoes, and onions we had to raise ourselves. For that we had a full-time gardener. The soil was very poor but a method had been worked out by some of the early missionaries to overcome that problem. The gardener spent much of his time making compost by burying leaves and other organic material until it rotted. Every month he would mix the rotting material the with dirt and move to another pit. After several months it would be ready for use. We had no other fertilizer and were using what later came to be called organic gardening.

The gardener would dig a trench about a foot wide and a foot or more deep and fill it with the compost, mixed with the surrounding soil. In that mixture he would plant the seeds and we would have good vegetables. We had very little loss to insects and it may have been because our plants were so healthy the local parasites were not familiar with them and left them alone. We also raised pineapples but although the pineapple patch was quite large we did not manage to salvage many of them for our own use because there was a path that ran from the hospital ran past our garden and visitors to the hospital helped themselves. We never objected to that.

Peanuts were available and we learned that making peanut butter is a very simple matter. All the cook had to do was grind the peanuts in the meat grinder until they had the right consistency and add a little salt. The kerosene refrigerator had a freezer so we could have plenty of ice, make ice cream and keep frozen any perishable food we happened to have. We were able to keep the milk we made from powdered milk, and a jug of ice water we enjoyed very much.

We could buy coffee locally, since the government was encouraging its cultivation. In Batetela society it was not customary for men to do much work. The husband would help in building the house and clearing a plot of land in the forest for a garden. From then on it was the responsibility of the woman to raise all the food, do all the cooking and take care of the children. The house cost almost nothing to build, there were no heating or electric or water bills to pay, so there was very little expense except for clothing. If a man did work most of the money could go for such luxuries as a bicycle, cloth, kerosene, beer, and jewelry.

That may sound like an ideal system from the man's point of view, but it was being upset because the government felt that if the country was going to be developed the men were going to have to go to work. For that reason the authorities tried to encourage the men to raise cash crops, such as coffee and cotton. The coffee they raised was Robusta, different from the Arabica sold in the United States but very good. The first time we bought some coffee beans from a local producer we gave them to the cook without knowing they have to be aged for at least a year to reduce the caffeine level. We did not sleep well for three nights and from then on we aged the beans before using them. We visited a plant that processed cotton and were told that the production was disappointing. Consumerism was slow in taking hold.

The boys were as happy as they could be. There was very little traffic so they had all the room they wanted to run and play and ride their bicycles up and down the road without danger. There were several boys about the same age so the did have someone to play with. They also had Congolese play-mates and were picking up the language more rapidly than we were. I heard Hari talking with Shuku and Shinga in the kitchen several times and he seemed perfectly at ease. One day when we were riding our bicycles along a path in the forest he astonished me by telling me the Otetela names of things we saw. As we rode along we saw a column of ants and I told him to be careful of the driver ants. He promptly replied that those were not driver ants, but were *alumbulumbu*, with a bite much worse than driver ants. Then we saw a bird he identified as a *dingwanga*. His pronunciation was perfect, like that of the other boys his age who had been there for several years. Paul was probably even more fluent in Otetela because he did not spend as much time in school and played most of the day with his Congolese friends. In good American fashion all the houses had lawns around them, creating a problem. Africans never had grass in the villages and the ground was swept clean every day so that the villages were always neat. One of the reasons for the exceptional cleanliness was a fear of snakes and a very rational fear it was. We tried to keep our lawn clipped short but with the heat and the rain it was a constant task. I bought a lawn mower in Luluabourg but it wore out in a few months and the students had to go back to cutting the grass with machetes. I soon learned that it is wiser to let the people do things their way in most cases rather than to try to change them.

Snakes were plentiful, mostly cobras, and the cat used to amuse himself by playing with them. He would come up close, taunt the snake, and then jump back when it struck. Cobras are not really dangerous if one sees them first because they cannot strike farther than their head is raised, usually not more than a foot. If we saw a snake we called one of the servants or students and he would kill it with a machete. If someone was bitten by a snake the doctor usually had an antidote. The exception was the black mamba, a large, very venomous creature with an aggressive personality that could move very quickly. One day we sighted one crossing the lawn and watched as it climbed a palm tree. The shotguns came out and firing into the top of the tree did not cease until we were sure it was dead.

There were many animals and creatures that were a nuisance but we rarely saw most of them because they were nocturnal, for which I was grateful, especially when it came to leopards and wildcats. One of the most annoying was the horse bat, so called because its face resembled that of a horse. It was

It took newcomers some time to become accustomed to the presence of so much wildlife, most of it in smaller sizes than gorillas.

Visitors were generally very well treated and honored because we had so few of them.

also called a fruit bat because it was fond of fruit, and when the mangoes were ripening they would come in large numbers to feed on the fruit in our trees while making an awful racket that kept us awake.

Just a word about the location of Wembo Nyama, the first mission station established for the Methodist Church in central Congo. Founded by Bishop Lambeth about 1914, it was then in the middle of nowhere. The bishop had come to the Congo and had visited other Christian mission societies, mostly Baptist and Presbyterian, that had been established along the Congo River and its tributaries so as to be close to the only means of transportation. He had set out on foot from Lusambo, heading northeast looking for a place to establish a mission. When he arrived in Batetela country a chief, Wembo Nyama by name, welcomed him and offered him a piece of land near the village known as Ewangu. The bishop applied to the Congo government and was duly given a concession consisting of a small plot of land for the establishment of the mission. The mission assumed responsibility for the evangelization of the Batetela tribe of about 200,000 members in an area slightly smaller than the state of Colorado. Many people still called the village Ewangu, because the original chief Wembo Nyama's successor had not been very popular. With thousands of acres of fertile rain forest to the north and miles of beautiful savannah to the south it seemed odd that the bishop had chosen that particular site, but perhaps it was all he could get. With swamps and streams in the shallow valley encircling the concession on three sides, there were fine breeding grounds for mosquitoes, tsetse flies, and other assorted vermin. It may not have been the best location in the area but it did have some advantages. There were plenty of springs for fresh water and the streams were used by the students and the local inhabitants for bathing.

Once the main station was established others were opened

in Lodja to the northwest, Katako Kombe due north, Minga in the south, and Tunda south east, which pretty well covered the territory assigned. Considering the difficulties of transportation, communications, health, and so on, founding a mission station anywhere in that area was a great accomplishment.

When I read articles complaining about how the schools in the United States do not have adequate facilities, I smile. In the Congo we learned that other things are more important than beautiful buildings and expensive equipment. The schools at Wembo Nyama, for there were several of them, were very basic. There was a primary school, a lower-level school for the training of teachers in the first three grades, and the monitors school whose graduates were qualified to teach in grades four through six. The *Ecole de Moniteurs* was, to borrow a term from the state university system, the flagship institution. At the hospital there was also an active program to train nurses and midwives.

All the buildings were austere but adequate. The students sat at desks with an attached bench wide enough for two students, just like the one we see in films of Dickens' novels. The blackboards were simply a patch of concrete painted black and there was one sixty-watt light bulb in each classroom so that students could study in the evening. There was no library and no gymnasium. The only sport was soccer, which the boys played barefoot with great skill and agility. The lack of modern facilities was partly due to the poverty of the mission and partly to the feeling among some of our colleagues that education for the natives was not necessary at all. In spite of such opposition and the lack of funding, those who did believe in education had managed to create a working school system with a minimum of resources. We also received a subsidy from the government for each teacher and student but that went mostly to support the boarding department. The tuition, including board, was 400 francs (eight dollars) a year.

Another thing that made our schools different from schools at home was a plan. There was a curriculum that prescribed very clearly what the pupils were to be taught in each subject at each grade level. The curriculum was not restrictive but only established minimum requirements beyond which a teacher could go if he had the time. We may not have had a winning football team but we knew where we were going. Because we knew exactly what each student was supposed to know, testing was easy and examinations were designed to tell us how much each student had learned. We were not allowed to teach English, so students who had had American teachers throughout their academic career could not speak a word of English.

We did have two things that made up for the physical deficiencies of the schools. One was discipline and the other was motivation. We never had serious discipline problems because the students were taught at home to respect those in a position of authority and if a student did break a rule he expected to be punished. Not all the children in the area had a strong desire for knowledge but those who did understood what they were doing and worked hard to achieve their goal. Our purpose was to train teachers for our primary schools that had the usual six years. Many of our students were several years older than students in the same grades in Europe or the United States. Some started school late and some missed a few years for one reason or another. Those who wanted to go on to further education could take an examination to enter the seventh year preparatory class, which was in the monitors school itself.

Competition for further training was very stiff because the monitors school was one of very few in the region offering education beyond elementary school. The Catholic mission at Tshombe Sainte Marie about forty miles away offered about the same opportunity. In addition to the monitors school we had another school called an *Ecole d'Apprentissage Pédagogique,* which took some of the students who could not qualify for the monitors school. Those students received two years of training and could teach in the first three years of primary school, mostly in the vernacular. They were important to maintaining the primary schools because they did not speak French well enough to go to the city to look for a job. Because of our limited resources we could not accommodate all the students who wanted more education and it was a source of frustration.

We would have 150 or more applications for forty vacancies in the seventh-year course and would administer an examination to determine which were the brightest and had the best background. We tested them in French, using a dictée, and other academic subjects, and then we used a fable by La Fontaine.

We would have them read the fable about the fox and the crow and then asked each of them to write a short essay telling us what the moral of the fable was. Since La Fontaine had borrowed the fable from Aesop, a Greek, we felt it had a universal quality and that people everywhere would understand it the same way. La Fontaine, by the way, collected hundreds of fables and retold them in elegant French verse.

The results of the essay test were extraordinary. Few of the applicants interpreted the fable the way a European would. We had all kinds of peculiar interpretations, indicating that the students had a somewhat different way of looking at things than we did. I would like to emphasize that we did not consider their mental processes in any way inferior—only different for cultural reasons. Anyone who has read the Uncle Remus stories by Joel Chandler Harris will remember how the smaller animal constantly outwitted the larger, stronger animal, and that cleverness and deceit were highly valued. Such stories are an important part of the folklore and oral literature of Africa.

Although we took in forty of what we considered to be the most promising students, we did have some attrition and at the end of five years we would graduate between ten and fifteen. Some found the work too difficult, some decided they did not want to be teachers and some left when they felt they had enough French to seek another career. Every year one student would be drafted into the *Force publique*, as the army was called. A Belgian administrator would come and have the boys line up so he could select one of them for military service. I found it amusing that although the Batetela had been known for their courage as warriors and their viciousness as agents for the Arab slave traders during the nineteenth century—raiding neighboring tribes without mercy for slaves—all of our students were terrified at the thought of military service. What made their fear more ridiculous was that those who were chosen were not assigned to units that might be involved in fighting, but because of their education would be used as clerks or teachers. They would also have opportunities for additional training which would prepare them for a more rewarding career than teaching in a village school. For anyone who had any ambition being drafted was the best thing that could happen to him.

The program at the monitors school was very intensive. The students rose before six o'clock in the morning, attended a prayer meeting soon after six and started classes at eight after taking care of various chores. They had no breakfast because that was not their custom. I did not attend the prayer meeting because the air in the morning was excessively damp and I was afraid it might not be good for my health. I consulted our Swedish doctor and after some reflection he agreed that since I had always lived in a dry climate like Colorado it would not be advisable for me to become active so early in the morning.

The academic part of the day ran until noon. We then had two hours during the hottest part of the day for lunch and an obligatory siesta because of the insalubrious climate. Afternoons were devoted to various practical courses such as carpentry, brickmaking, gardening, and building construction, all skills the administration thought a village teacher should have. In theory it was a very good program because it would enable the teachers to contribute to raising the standard of living of the rural population.

When we first arrived one of the Wamamas was the director of the school. She was in charge of administration and supervising the boarding department and she taught several classes. The rest of the faculty consisted of Jackie and me, the agriculture teacher, one young single lady, and two Congolese teachers, Luhahi and Kasongo. I went to the school at eight o'clock and taught French and geography until noon. Jackie had to teach our older son, who had just entered first grade, using the Calvert method of home schooling. She also had one other pupil and had class until ten. Then the two boys went to the home of the other boy for two more hours of school and Jackie went to the lower-level teacher training school where she taught pedagogy and to the primary school where she taught music, all in Otetela.

She also taught music, pedagogy, and psychology in the monitors school in French, and she had two piano students. Because she was teaching in Otetela and working with women, few of whom spoke any French at all, she learned Otetela more rapidly than I did and in much greater depth. If I spoke Otetela with any of my students they would reply in French and ask me to speak French so my vocabulary was limited to what was needed to communicate with laborers and villagers to get work done or buy food for the school. I really wanted to learn Otetela but, on reflection, I thought the students were right and I was not there to learn Otetela but to teach them French.

Fernand, the young agriculture teacher, did his best to teach better methods of farming and gardening. He had a very productive garden that the students worked in as part of their training and he conducted various experiments looking for new ideas. His innovations, if adopted, would have improved the diet of the local people considerably. The single lady who had been teaching arts and crafts to the girls in the elementary school left soon after we arrived and I inherited the small building she had and the equipment, including a potter's wheel and loom which were less appropriate for the boys in the monitors school than they had been for the girls. Given our shortage of space, it was a welcome addition and was put to good use. The teaching of arts and crafts was one of my responsibilities, along with the supervision of brickmaking, construction of housing for married students and other buildings we might need.

For each course the students had a notebook with fifty pages in it. When the notebooks were distributed the first thing the students did was number the pages to prevent them from using them for anything else. That seemed strange at first but the rules and procedures had been established by people with years of experience so I did not consider it prudent to question anything. It was a useful system because much of what they were learning was written in the notebooks, having been copied from the blackboard. Homework assignments were also written in the notebooks and handed in to the teacher for correction. At the end of the year each student had a miniature library in case he wished to look up something.

We knew that with few exceptions our students had no intention of staying in a village teaching school. We were not so naïve as to believe they were really interested in spending their whole life in the service of their people when there were so many other opportunities. There was such a demand for Congolese who could speak French and had some education that after a year or two of teaching, when a teacher felt he had repaid the mission for his education, he would quietly slip away and go to the city to find a job that paid many times what he was paid as a teacher. In a way they could not be blamed for leaving, but it did make it difficult for us to maintain a good village school system. There were two things that worked against us. One was the quality of education and the other was the family system. Everyone had many relatives in the extended family as it is called, which has many advantages, but in that large family there were very few members at that time who actually earned any money. So, when a young man started getting a regular paycheck he had relatives, mostly uncles, constantly asking for money and it was almost impossible for him to refuse. Consequently, he was always broke and had nothing to show for his years of hard work. One way to escape from the burden of family obligations was to go as far as possible from home, and many did for that reason.

Another reason was the quality of education the students received. The mission policy of setting a very high standard of moral and ethical behavior paid off for the students as well as the school. One day a student pointed out to me that at the Catholic school they had electric lights in the dormitories, better food and all kinds of material advantages. I told him, and others, if they thought they could get a better education there to go ahead. None left. They knew that even though conditions were harsh in our school the Protestant schools had the reputation of turning out graduates who were morally superior and they were proud to be part of that.

It is possible to deplore the strictness of the mission with its demanding schedule but the result was good for the students. Our graduates did not drink or smoke, did not get into trouble and were known to be honest and dependable. That is not something I have just imagined. We had too many reports of actual cases where employers would openly express a preference for Protestants. We also had many letters from businessmen asking us to send them one of our graduates. We could never comply with their requests because so few graduates remained in the area and those we wanted to keep because they were so valuable.

The discipline was very strict and at first I did not understand why, but as time went on, and particularly later when I became director of the school, I realized there was a purpose in it. The students had a strange attitude and seemed to feel more secure when they were strictly controlled. If a student did something wrong and was not punished for it he just was not happy; he was dissatisfied until he received punishment to restore the balance. When that happened there was a visible change in the student and he looked as though he had just had a heavy burden lifted from his shoulders.

Conduct in the classroom was excellent, which made teaching a really rewarding experience. As soon as the teacher walked into the room the students stood up and remained standing until told to sit. They all paid attention in class, they always did their homework and were always obedient. It was an ideal teaching situation.

For the primary school we had to print the books that were used in our own print shop because the instruction was in Otetela. Since Otetela was not one of the languages designated as a lingua franca like Swahili or Lingala the government did not print books in that language. The lead type was set by hand and the printing was done on an old hand-fed press, a machine that has become very rare. For the monitors school we used many of the same books that were used in Belgium for French, math, science, history, geography, and so forth.

There was an amusing story about how in the beginning the French had used the same books in Africa that were used in France and students had a history book that started out, "*Nos ancêtres les Gaulois avaient les yeux bleus et les cheveux blonds.*" In English that means "Our ancestors, the Gauls, had blue eyes and blond hair." which was hardly appropriate for students in Senegal or the Congo. As a reader we had a set of books written for use in West Africa which had stories about Mamadou and Binetta, two West African teenagers, and although there were significant differences in the culture they were enough similarities to make them relevant.

Discipline problems were very rare and most of them did not really have anything to do with what went on in the classroom. If something had to be done to relieve the student of guilt and to show him that we meant business, we have various punishments to suit different levels of dereliction which could be carried out without supervision. For example, we were building a tennis court for the Ewangu Heights Racquet Club, as we called the informal group who met to play tennis between the time we finished work and the time the sun went down—which was always with a few minutes of six o'clock because of our proximity to the equator. On the prairie south of the mission compound there were millions of mushroom-shaped black anthills. Those anthills, after they had been soaked and crushed, made a superb surface for a tennis court. It was hard enough to play on but a little spongy so that it was easy on the feet and also porous enough that when we had twenty or thirty inches of rain in a day the water would all soak through without damaging the surface, so we could play on it the next day. If a student did something that was not too serious he would have to bring in fifty anthills, using the cart equipped with automobile tires we had at the school. He would bring in the anthills and dump them by the tennis court. We had a worker whom we paid to soak the anthills and crush them with the center rib of a palm branch and then pound them smooth. The result was a fine tennis court except that we had no fence as a backstop and no ball boys to chase balls. For the lines we used pure kaolin, a white clay used to make porcelain.

For more serious infractions we had a more onerous punishment. All over Africa there are huge red anthills, some of them more than six feet high. In each one, far underneath, was a queen ant, happily laying thousand of eggs which would later develop into large red ants. The anthills in our area were almost as hard as concrete, so digging into them involved much very hard work. If a student was guilty of a major infraction we would ask him to bring in the queen ant from a particular anthill. It was a practical sort of punishment, because he would have to spend his precious free time for the next week or two digging in the anthill until he found the queen ant. It was useful as a punishment because it required no supervision and was very effective. Fortunately, it was rarely used. I did not enjoy imposing harsh punishment on any of the students, but it was what they expected and doing otherwise would be showing signs of weakness that would lead to a loss of respect.

Almost all the students in the monitors school were boarding, so we had dormitories and a dining hall with its own kitchen. Most of the students were older than high school students in other countries and some were in their early twenties and married. Each of the married students had a house like those in the villages and their wives were enrolled in some sort of training course conducted by the Wamamas. The single boys were housed two to a room in a long building. They all ate their one daily meal in the dining hall, having rice or millet, depending on the season, garnished with manioc greens that looked like creamed spinach and covered with palm oil.

That they ate rice was unusual because rice is not normally grown in most of Africa. The rice was not the kind that is raised in paddies in Asia or California. It was what is called upland or dry land rice and grew very well in central Congo, but its production was very labor intensive. To plant the rice the husband and wife would clear a small patch of forest, removing all the trees and other vegetation, after which the rice would be planted in the humus-rich soil. For a year or two the soil was very rich and there was a good crop, but after the second year the land was no longer fertile and another piece of forest would have to be cleared. It was a very destructive practice because once the fertility, the result of centuries of soil-building, was gone it was gone forever. I was told by someone who had been there a very long time that during the last forty years a strip of forest thirty miles wide had been almost completely destroyed, leaving only small patches of forest dispersed on the savannah. Millet, on the other hand, was planted on the savannah and apparently did not require as fertile soil as rice, so the boys ate rice half the year and millet the other half.

That meant that we had to buy enough grain at the time of harvest or soon after to last for six months. We had no refrigeration and no storage facilities that were secure enough from insects and other pests, but a simple and practical way to store grain had been figured out. There were no service stations in the area, so each of us had to buy our own gasoline in fifty-gallon drums from a Portuguese trader who delivered. We kept the drum on a rack and when we needed to fill the car's tank we would tip up the lower end and pour two or three gallons into a bucket. Then, using a funnel and an old felt hat for a strainer we would fill the tank. Straining was essential because many of the drums had rust or other impurities inside and a felt hat was the only strainer fine enough to get them all out. Consequently, we always had a good supply of empty drums we could use for storage.

After cleaning the barrels very thoroughly we would put them over a fire to make sure that all the moisture had been evaporated, fill them with grain, put in a piece of cotton soaked in a chemical solution that would kill any bugs, and screw on the lid. If we were out of the chemical we would place a small lighted candle inside and screw on the lid. The candle would consume all the oxygen and the bugs would die.

The daily meal for the students was prepared in a dark, dingy building just big enough for the two enormous cast-iron pots like the ones featured in cartoons about explorers and cannibals, one for the rice or millet and one for the *djese*, or manioc greens, or meat if the cook had it. The manioc greens were very nutritious and with the addition of palm oil, which is very rich, the diet was adequate even though to us it seemed very monotonous. The boys would also snack on fruit during the day but did not consider that a meal.

There were no shops where we could buy groceries in the quantities needed to feed eighty boys; only a few shops in the neighboring village whose stock was limited to the immediate needs of the villagers. That meant that someone had to spend a lot of time going out to the villages almost every week to buy food. The first two years we were there the director, one of the Wamamas, would go out with one of the teachers and her pickup truck and buy what was needed. The second two years when I was also the director I was responsible for buying the food. I was not allowed to use the pickup truck or the large mission truck, which would have been too large anyway, to make the task easier, but the spirit of cooperation I thought would prevail on a mission station did not extend to personal possessions. Fortunately, with a little ingenuity we were able to devise a trailer hitch and adapt the cart we had so that it could be used as a trailer. Once or twice a week we would hook it up behind the Chevrolet and drive to the surrounding villages with an African assistant, usually a student, to find the destination and help with the purchasing. They always seemed to know exactly where we could find enough rice or millet to make the trip worthwhile. Those short trips were interesting and educational because I was able to visit villages I would not have seen otherwise, some of which had hardly been touched by civilization as evidenced by the attire of the inhabitants. The farther they were from the mission station or a government post the less they wore because first of all no one had told them to change their habits, and secondly they had almost no cash income so they could not normally afford store-bought clothing or even much cloth.

There was one exception. Every year well-meaning people would send out a barrel or large box of secondhand clothing that had been collected so that the natives would have something to cover their nakedness. The garments were sold to the people for just a few cents each so they were within the reach of almost everyone. The purchasers had no idea what the original use of the clothing was so it was not unusual to see a man proudly wearing a woman's pink chenille bathrobe or, what was the most popular, a bright uniform jacket with the words *Roxy Theater* or *Hilton Hotel* on a shoulder patch or on the breast pocket. The women rarely sported such finery, being satisfied with the traditional piece of cloth.

When we arrived in a village we would find the local drummer and tell him what we wanted to buy, which often included something other than rice or millet. The Batetela talking drum was a wonderful instrument. Wedge-shaped, it was about thirty-six inches long and four inches wide at the top, slightly shorter and eight inches wide at the bottom, and about twenty-four inches high. It was carved from a single piece of wood, and along almost the entire length of the top there was a slit about three-quarters of an inch wide through which the carver skillfully hollowed it out so that it had six distinct tones, three on each side. I watched a carver working on one. He had a sharp blade attached to a long stick and was patiently removing the wood from the inside in small strips until he had the right tone. The drummer would suspend the drum by means of a cord that passed around his neck in such a way that he could beat both sides of the drum at the same time. The drums were passed from father to son and being a drummer carried quite a bit of prestige.

We were told that the drummers could communicate any message and that at the time of the death of King Albert of the

Belgians in 1934 the news reached the interior by drum before it arrived on the telegraph. I could well believe that because when we left Léopoldville we had sent a telegram to Lodja to advise the people there of our arrival. When we arrived in Lodja the postmaster asked us if we were going out to the mission and if we were would we please deliver a telegram. It was the one we had sent more than ten days earlier. If the story about King Albert was correct, and we had no reason to doubt it, it meant that the system of communication operated across tribal lines even though the various tribes were often hostile to each other.

About half an hour after the drummer beat out his message, which could be heard a great distance away, the women would come strolling in from their gardens with rice, millet, plantains, bananas, peas, and whatever else we had asked for in baskets perched on their heads. We would hang a Roman scale from a tree branch, weigh each basket, and pay the seller. There was very little haggling and the transactions were carried out in a pleasant, relaxed atmosphere. Once we had bought everything we wanted we would load up the trailer and drive back to the mission. None of the roads were paved and many consisted of a path through the tall grass that was hard to see. There was one village I liked to go to because the people there made the most beautiful raffia baskets and trays. I always bought as many as I could. I tried having a village teacher buy rice for us but it did not work out very well because somehow it ended up costing us more for the rice than we usually paid.

On Sundays the students had meat with their meal. It was a real treat because in their home village they probably did not have meat that often. Making sure we had meat on Sunday was sometimes a problem. One time we were able to buy a truckload of dried fish from Lake Tanganyika from some traders who were passing through. The fish were smaller than sardines but the boys liked them so that solved the problem for several weeks. We bought them by weight and were surprised to find when we emptied the sacks someone had carelessly left some gravel in them. Ordinarily, the meat we served had been bought from local hunters who would bring in all kinds of wild game, including hippopotamus, wild boar, antelope, and so on. Sometimes it was so rotten I could not get within twenty feet, but the odor never bothered the students and I left it to someone else to decided on its suitability. They were accustomed to eating meat that was considerably overripe by our standards.

No matter what was available it occasionally happened that a student would come to me and say, "Uwandji, I cannot eat that." Naturally, for him we would find something else because we wanted all our diners to be satisfied. He did not use the word totem but we assumed that we meant it was his totem animal or something like that. Each clan or subtribe appeared to have a totem animal, and if a member of that clan ate the meat of that animal he would become deathly ill and perhaps die. This actually happened, and was not just superstition. Scientists probably scoff at the idea, but my acceptance of their belief was reinforced by the fact that my own son Paul cannot eat duck, being allergic to it. He has tried African duck, Peking duck, and American duck, and the result is always the same.

One day I found out that Mr. Moyes, a Scottish missionary in Lusambo who acted as a trader and agent for those who lived far from the river like us, had cases of canned horse meat and gravy. It was not dog food but rather very good meat. Since no one in our area had ever had a horse as his totem animal, there not being any horses in the region, it helped solve the problem of Sunday dinner. After all, Europeans do not share the American prejudice against eating horse meat, and there are butcher shops in France called *boucheries chevalines* that sell nothing but horse meat. Also available were sausages similar to wieners, but we did not buy any of those because they were sold in cans with a picture of a young African on the label and the local people believed that the sausages were actually human fingers.

There were some popular delicacies we were reluctant to try. The flying ants were termites and larger than ordinary ants. During a certain season of the year they would leave the anthill and swarm, flying to a new location in large numbers. At that time the local people would cover the anthills with palm branches to catch as many as possible for snacks. Jackie and I never tried them but we understood that the boys did and liked them. There was no logical reason for not doing so because we eat shrimp and squid and consider snails a delicacy, but that was something we did not learn to do as children and we all have our cultural prejudices. Another local specialty we did not find appetizing was the palm worm, found in old, rotting palm trees. They were about an inch long, dirty yellow, and half an inch in diameter, resembling a hairless caterpillar. The doctor, who had more scientific curiosity, tried them and found them delicious. He said that when they had been fried all the gooey stuff inside disappeared and the outer coating had the consistency of thick bacon. He brought us some one day, praising the nut-like flavor, so we were obliged to try them. I had to admit that they did taste good but we could not overcome our feelings about eating such things. We had the same problem in Europe with tripe and what they called *filet américain*, a dish consisting of spiced, raw ground beef. There is always something in a foreign culture that takes some getting used to, like the sheep's eyeballs served to honored visiting guests in the Middle East and North Africa. The best defense is to claim dietary restrictions based on either religion or medical advice.

CHAPTER 8

How we communicate with the outside world through
MAS. We start to raise chickens. School activities.

THERE WERE OTHER THINGS going on aside from the monitors school. At the far end of the compound, which I never had
occasion to visit, was the girls' home for young women whose
parents wanted them to have a modern education.

The girls attended the primary school and then had training in other appropriate areas, such as sewing and hygiene and
that sort of thing. The future was bright for at least some of the
girls because a young man who had received a good education
would be more inclined to take a wife who could read and
write with him to the city than an illiterate village girl who
would find it difficult to adjust to city life. The only time I saw
the girls was after school let out and they went flying down the
road like a flight of birds.

The older ones often had blouses made of very sheer material and brassieres of the most garish printed cloth imagin-
able, colors and designs representing what some white manufacturer thought they should have. Any fabric made by the
Africans themselves was usually in much better taste. I thought
the funds spent on cloth could have been used more wisely to
buy the girls shoes, which only cost forty francs a pair. The
native costume, which consisted simply of a piece of cloth that
covered from the armpits to just above the knees when
wrapped around the body, was much more suitable and less
provocative than the attempts to imitate European dress.

Very few of the girls went beyond primary school and
those who did were trained as nurses or midwives under the

guidance of the hospital staff. We had a Belgian nurse and an American nurse who did an excellent job of training nurses, both male and female, to work in the hospital and to run rural clinics in remote villages. The rural clinic nurses could administer first aid, treat common ailments such as malaria, and send to the hospital those who needed care the nurse could not provide.

The dream of the single ladies was to have some of their girls graduate from the monitors school and become teachers or go on to a regular secondary school. Conditions have probably changed by now, but at that time they ran up against a firmly established custom that was hard to overcome. Girls in other cultures often do not have a clear idea of what their role in society is and are consequently torn between a desire to have a successful career in business or industry and simply being a wife and a mother. But Batetela girls knew exactly what they wanted to do and that was to get married as soon as possible and have children. I wondered how they felt about the single ladies because their way of life must have seemed a little unnatural to the girls, but maybe it did not.

We did have one girl who was doing quite well and managed to get to the third year of the monitors school. It looked as though she was going to make it, then one day we noticed that she was letting her hair grow. All the girls in the school had their heads shaved so we took her action as subtle way of letting us know that her plans had changed. We were all sad but there was nothing we could do about it and we wished her well. With a high infant mortality rate and so many health hazards it was understandable that reproduction was extremely important in that society.

Both Jackie and I were fully occupied during the day and spent most evenings after dinner during the week grading papers and preparing lesson plans. Saturday was almost free but that was the day the MAS truck came in from Lusambo with our mail. I believe MAS stood for *Messagerie automobilière du Sankuru*. It was a large covered stake-bodied truck that carried passengers, mail, and any other kind of cargo from Lusambo to Katako Kombe every Saturday, with a stop at Wembo Nyama on the way. The next day it returned to Lusambo so we had until late Sunday morning to read our mail and write our letters. That was also the day Paul became important. The young man who received the mail from the MAS truck was thoughtful enough to entrust to Paul the task of distributing the mail. Wherever he was when the truck came in he would stop what he was doing and say, "I've got to go to work now."

If we needed stamps or wanted to order something we would simply put the cash in an envelope addressed to the postmaster and send it on its way. One time I was not sure of the postage so I put on a little extra to make sure the letter would reach its destination. The next week the letter was returned with a note saying I had put too much postage on it. I thought the postmaster had been there too long. We thought it remarkable that we could conduct all our transactions in cash and receive so many kinds of packages from the United States or elsewhere with very little loss. The postmaster was the only white man in the post office, all the rest being Congolese. The mail service was very good and a few times we received air mail letters from home that only took a week.

The boys had a life that Huckleberry Finn would have envied. After a few hours of school they had the rest of the day to play with the other missionary children or with their African friends. Once we were well established the boys became interested in gardening and with the help of the gardener each one developed his own garden, which he tended with great care. Hari, being older, was very serious about his garden and was very pleased when we had some of his produce for dinner. He raised bananas, manioc, millet, peanuts, corn, sweet potatoes, and melons. He also found a pile of bricks in the yard and built a small house out by the laundry shed. Paul spent most of his time in the forest with his Congolese friends.

One day we noticed that the boys had nothing to wear. We asked them why and were told that they had given away almost all their shirts and shorts to their friends, a kind thing to do but it left them very short of clothing. We sent off an order to our parents and while we waited for the shipment to reach us we had a local tailor make them some shirts and shorts out of a local cloth called merikani, a very durable off-white cotton cloth. We pointed out that while generosity was a virtue it could be overdone.

We cleaned out the chicken house, dusted it liberally with DDT to kill the mites that plagued the chickens, repaired the fence and were in the chicken business. We soon had enough eggs for our own use and an occasional chicken for dinner. The native chickens were small and scrawny because the Africans didn't feed them. European chickens were much larger but were less resistant to disease, so the best policy was to cross the imported chickens with the local chickens. I had never raised chickens, but it did not take us long to learn how. We obtained a Rhode Island Red rooster from Lodja, and from time to time we were able to get other imported cocks from Luluabourg, so our flock was made up of poultry of an acceptable size in good health. Feed was no problem and did not cost much. The chickens were all free to forage in the spacious chicken yard and about once a week we would send someone out to the plain south of the mission to collect the same black anthills we were using for the tennis court. They were teeming with white larvae inside so once they were broken the chickens had a feast to supplement their usual diet of rice and millet.

Much of the feed came from the school kitchen. I noticed that every day one of the boys would pound the rice or millet with a pole in a mortar made by hollowing out the end of a log. The grain would then be sifted and the outer coating, or bran, would be discarded. Seeing that it was simply being thrown away, I arranged to have it brought instead to our chicken yard.

Fernand had the soil analyzed and had a white powder prepared that contained most of the minerals that were lacking. By adding a spoonful of mineral supplement to the bran we gave our chickens an excellent, balanced diet. The supplement was available free of charge to anyone who wanted it, but since the idea of feeding chickens or any animal was foreign to them, few of the Africans, aside from possibly a few of those who worked for us on the mission, took advantage of it.

Some of the people who saw how beautiful our chickens were asked us to sell them a cock and we did a few times. We also gave them eggs to have hatched under their own hens, but the results were always disappointing because the chickens were neither properly fed nor protected from predators. Even though we would explain why our chickens were larger and healthier, they always believed it was because of some sort of magic. We also had our problems with predators—snakes, wildcats, leopards, and possibly some of the two-legged variety. Somehow they all seemed to know when we had increased our flock and raided the chicken yard. We also had a few ducks, but they were less satisfactory than the chickens because they were terribly messy and Paul was allergic to them.

Another reason people believed that our success was due to occult science was when a disease called *djomotoy* swept through the region killing a great many chickens, we never lost any and it was futile to try to explain the real reason, that better nutrition made them resistant to disease. We did have one other small problem with raising our own chickens as a source of food. The boys would become attached to them as individuals and when one of the roosters was selected for dinner one of them would cry, "But he was my friend." It was sad but inevitable, because there can only be one adult cock in a chicken yard. If there are two they will fight until one is killed.

When we had not been there very long someone gave us a monkey named *Mauvaise*, which means bad, and a suitable name it was. He seemed to be fond of me and would jump up on my shoulder, and in his enthusiasm he would lose control and I would have to go in and change my shirt. He was a real problem because we did not know what to do with him. We could not have him in the house because he was not house-broken, and he had destructive tendencies. We could just let him run free, but that would not do because one day he went next door and carefully removed all the blossoms from the potted plants on our neighbor's front porch. We did not want to put him in a cage even if we could have had one made, and if we kept him restrained with a very long leash so that he could make his home in the breadfruit tree behind the house, a leopard or a wildcat would get him. We finally took him out to the forest and let him go. He seemed as happy as we were to terminate the relationship.

We finally reached the end of our first semester of teaching and a week of examinations that had the students properly terrified. Examination time was very important to the students because passing the exams carried more weight than it does in the American system. We had to give exams in everything except drawing, so I spent a lot of time preparing tests that would be fair in French and geography, while Jackie worked on her tests in pedagogy and music. I had one student who refused to believe that the earth was round but he still passed geography. The week after the examinations we had to grade everything, including the notebooks the students were required to keep, following the European tradition. We also had to discuss the results with the students on an individual basis, a time-consuming but very productive exercise because it showed each student what he needed to work on.

We were supposed to have a long vacation during the summer, but the government had decided to change the school year to coincide with the school year in Belgium, so for the next three years the vacations were to be shortened, the transition being made gradually. Right after the examinations had been dealt with I had a chance to visit Katako Kombe. I had never been there and was glad to have the opportunity. The trip was being made for the purpose of delivering a load of cement to the mission there and to pick up a large amount of rice and other commodities all at one time and be able to use the mission truck.

Unlike Wembo Nyama, which was situated on a low, wooded plateau, Katako Kombe was on a hilltop with a magnificent view in every direction. The superior site, like that of Lodja, must have had something to do with the presence of a government post that had been there for more than fifty years. The early administrators had plenty of time to select the best locations and usually did. Off to the north we could see the equatorial forest, a dark, gloomy place stretching for hundreds of miles across the equator. In other directions there were beautiful plains with enough wild game to provide for fairly good hunting, or so I was told. I never saw any wild game anywhere and it certainly was not as plentiful there as it was in Kenya and Tanganyika.

Between the two stations there were patches of forest but they were not quite the same as the real rain forest. Being a newer station, Katako Kombe was smaller than Wembo Nyama but it had a good school, a beautiful church, very comfortable housing for the missionaries and a dispensary that was not quite as large as the hospital at Wembo Nyama. There was no doctor there, only a nurse trained by the mission, but that was enough because there was a government hospital in the town. The next morning we set out for Luhata, a village about fifteen kilometers off the main road and about one-fourth of the way back to Wembo Nyama. One of the missionaries in Katako Kombe had made arrangements for us to buy rice and had left sacks and scales so that the teacher and the pastor could weigh the rice brought in by the villagers. When we arrived we found over two tons all ready to buy, a wonderful thing because it would save us many trips to villages near the mission. I sat at a little table under a shed erected for the purpose of providing shelter for the rice buyer. As the teacher read off the names of the sellers they came forward and I paid them. As each one received his money he was encouraged by the teacher and the chief of the village to make a contribution to the church. While some seemed reluctant to part with five francs or so, most of them gave willingly. The money stayed in the village, probably to contribute to the support of the pastor.

When we had all our barrels and sacks filled we began to buy djese, or manioc greens, an important part of the daily meal. Then I bought several hundred pounds of manioc and one basket of peanuts for our own use to make peanut butter. The students would not eat manioc unless there was nothing else because it was very bland and less nutritious than grain. Since manioc and corn were introduced into Africa from America by the Portuguese, I wondered what the Africans ate before they had contact with the outside world.

We thought it was about time to go to the dentist, so we made arrangements to visit Lubondai on the Presbyterian mission not far from Luluabourg. Bob, the young man from Denver who ran the print shop, and Fernand went with us. Traveling in the Congo involved more than simply throwing a few things into a suitcase. First of all we had to grease and check the car over thoroughly following the instructions in the shop manual from the factory. Then we had to fill the tank, carefully straining the gasoline. We had to make sure we had enough food to last us all the time we were gone and a generous supply of boiled and filtered drinking water, a small Primus stove to cook on in case we had to stay somewhere where there were no cooking or catering facilities, a set of car

118

tools, an ax, and a machete for fallen trees across the road, and a small shovel.

We set out early one morning and drove to Lusambo where we enjoyed the hospitality of Mr. Moyes, the Scottish missionary. We had hoped to stay in one of the cottages the mission had at Lake Munkamba, but we found that they were fully booked so we stayed in a hotel in Luluabourg one night before going on to Lubondai. Our visit there was pleasant, we all had our dental problems solved, and we visited the secondary school at Mutoto where we found some of our graduates employed as teachers. We enjoyed seeing Luluabourg again, especially the ice cream parlor, and it was important for the boys because they had been longing to go to the big city. We were also able to do a little shopping and returned home happy and refreshed.

Soon after school started I took over the arts and crafts classes the curriculum required one afternoon a week. Before coming out I had promised one of my teachers at the University of Denver that I would not teach perspective in Africa. Like many romantic artists, she apparently had the idea that doing so would destroy the students' ability to express themselves in a way that was completely consistent with their culture, whatever that might be. We did try drawing simple objects but none of the students showed any interest in drawing so I did not have to worry about perspective. Instead of trying to turn out painters in the limited time we had, I tried to find areas that might interest them and be useful at the same time.

In their language the words for colors were extremely vague, even more vague than those used by decorators and paint manufacturers. There are words that describe colors in precise terms such as cobalt blue and burnt umber, but they are only used by artists. Printers also have a system of identifying colors by a universally understood system of numbers. In Otetela the same word was used for all cool colors like blue or green and another word included all shades of red brown and orange, and there were words for black and white. They learned the French words for the primary and secondary colors, which colors went together in various color schemes, how colors can be light and dark, but we had neither the time nor the need to go further. Later, when I saw the awful gouache paintings being done in Léopoldville by Congolese artists under the guidance of some European who taught them that was the way Africans should paint I felt justified in not teaching them to paint.

Some of the houses had beautiful geometric designs on the walls, but they seemed old and while they made fine hut decorations I did not want the students to just copy them. They had been done in earth colors, using the various colors traditional in Africa. It appeared that the best thing to do was to base the course on familiar things, using available materials. In Luluabourg I had bought a Bakuba carved box suitable for keeping pens and pencils on a desk. I got a piece of fairly soft wood which was just right for carving and made a copy of it with carving tools I had ordered from England, decorating the top with the same simple carved design. Then I asked each student to make a similar box. They responded with enthusiasm although wood carving was not as important a part of their culture as it was with the Bakuba who decorated everything they used. The Bakuba, also known as the Bushongo, also carved drinking cups in the shape of a head as a carryover from their former custom of drinking from the skull of a vanquished enemy to absorb some of his vital force. The students did so well with the boxes that they moved on to carving miniature stools, copies eight or ten inches high of the stools used in the villages. That project was successful too, but I did not go so far as to ask them to carve the figurines, called fetishes, that had been part of their culture but which were rarely used any more by the Batetela and other tribes in the region. The Basonge, the

Baluba, and other tribes in the Congo basin produced some great masterpieces, but Batetela carving was not very good. Such objects were considered by outsiders to be "idols" that were worshipped but they were not. They were simply used to house a spirit whose purpose was to protect them from evil, which is quite a different thing.

The most successful crafts project was the making of wicker furniture. There was a very skilled craftsman, a victim of polio, who was paralyzed from the waist down and was employed to teach his craft to the students as he had being doing for years. He was an excellent teacher and was respected by the students. All the materials were available in the forest and the students knew where to find them so no cost was involved. They made chairs and tables and other useful items they could either keep for themselves or sell because there was a good demand for well-made furniture. None of the students planned to follow furniture making as a career but the program did fit in with the plan to introduce what might become successful cottage industries in the rural areas.

We carefully avoided anything that had any affinity with the ebony or ivory elephants or other hideous airport art. We only used the fairly soft wood that had always been used for masks and fetishes and household objects and we only used designs that were traditional among the Batetela or neighboring tribes. There was a young carver who lived near the mission and needed work. I gave him a fine set of English carving tools and had him make a copy of a Basonge mask I had. Then I asked him to do a figurine of the Bula Matadi. He produced a beautiful carving of the administrator with a little pith helmet perched on his head, a bush jacket and shorts, but following the typically African proportions which call for one third for the head and neck, one third for the body and one third for the legs and feet. I then had him do some more carvings of students, which had the same proportions and were very amusing.

CHAPTER 9

We add a building to the school for arts and crafts. How we got our building materials. Jackie starts to improve the music in the church. Our experiences with ferries.

THE SMALL BUILDING that had been used for arts and crafts had a loom and a potter's wheel. The loom we never used because we knew nothing about weaving and also because none of the students would have had the time. The potter's wheel we did use later on. There was also a drafting table in one corner and a filing cabinet, so I used that corner for my office. The office in the main classroom building hardly had enough room for the school clerk. There was not enough room in the crafts building for more than six or eight students to sit around the table that took up most of the center of the room.

It was certainly not adequate for doing wood carving or furniture making, so we decided to build a proper shed that would also have room for the school carpenter's shop and a blacksmith's forge.

We selected a site and had our crew of laborers bring in enough poles for the roof so we could start building. The structure was to be a fairly large open shed with a thatched roof and an enclosed area at one end for the storage of tools and equipment. We did not want to follow the traditional wattle and daub type of construction because we wanted something that would last a long time so we chose an alternative, bricks. There was plenty of good clay available and the mission had a brick plant that could turn out several thousand neat wire-cut bricks a day, but those bricks were reserved for a hospital that was to be built some day, a garage for the mission truck, a new house for the engineer in charge of building the hospital, and a guest house for the increasing number of travelers who were coming through and had no place else to stay. The school was so far down the list of priorities that if we were to have any new buildings at all we would have to depend on our own resources.

We had access to an antique hand-operated brick press that had been used for the construction of the church and the school and several houses before the modern brick plant had been installed. We set it up near a good clay deposit and began to make bricks two at a time, as part of our crafts program. Two boys with shovels would fill the forms with clay and then two boys pulled on a long lever to compress the clay in the form. Then two other boys carried the bricks to an area where they were left to dry. A crew of five or six students working several hours a day could make as many as 1,500 bricks a week. The students did not appear to mind the hard work and made it easier by setting up a rhythmic chant which seemed to make it easier. When working together Africans tend to establish a rhythm that is not only pleasant to listen to but serves to make the work less arduous. On large construction jobs it was customary to hire a drummer to provide accompaniment while the men worked. Once the bricks were pressed they were put out in the sun to dry because if they contained moisture they could explode during the firing. The drying took about a month. While waiting for the bricks to dry we had to collect wood for the firing, and when we had enough bricks we stacked them up, leaving a place at the bottom for the fire. It took three or four days to fire them and during that time we had to have someone at the kiln around the clock. It was a long and difficult process.

Looking for a better solution, we decided to try adobe bricks such as those used in Arizona and New Mexico. One of the older missionaries told me had seen adobe bricks used farther south where there was much less rain, but that the bricks had cement mixed with the dirt. New Mexico and Arizona have less than twelve inches of rainfall a year and central Congo must have had more than 100 inches. One of my duties was to measure the rainfall every day and there were many days that the rainfall at Wembo Nyama exceeded twelve inches.

At such times it was not like an ordinary rain with separate drops but rather a solid wall of water that came down all at once. The rain did not usually last very long and when it was over all the water soaked into the ground or ran off into the surrounding streams and the air somehow seemed fresher than before.

Because of the heavy rainfall, plain adobe bricks would not do even though the soil seemed to compact well. We decided it would be a good idea to add some cement to the soil, so we made test bricks with varying proportions of cement to dirt: one to ten, one to fifteen, and one to twenty. We then left the adobe bricks out in the rain for several months and found that the bricks with one part of cement to ten parts of dirt had hardly disintegrated at all, while the others had. From then on we used our adobe bricks instead of fired clay bricks. We wanted the storeroom to have plenty of light but to be secure at the same time, so we made some wooden molds in which we cast cement tiles in the form of a hollow hexagon with walls about an inch thick. Then when the walls of the storeroom were about five feet high we replaced bricks with the tiles, making a grill that admitted light and was at the same time strong and decorative.

For our new arts and crafts shed and other projects such as housing for married students and for furniture we also needed lumber. The mission had a modern sawmill with a five-foot blade that would handle the largest logs brought in on the mission truck, but all the lumber produced was reserved for the hospital and other high priority projects. We had to find some other way to get lumber and I was again impressed with the ability of the school staff and the students to solve problems. One day they produced a crew of three men who were not employees of the mission but were rather independent contractors who offered to supply us with lumber. They would go out into the forest with a fifteen-foot pit saw, axes, and shovels, and cut down a tree several feet in diameter. After it had fallen they would dig a pit underneath it. Then one man would go down into the pit and another would stand on top of the tree trunk. Each one would take hold of his end of the saw and they would proceed to saw the tree into planks. It was extremely hard work but it apparently paid fairly well and the men could work at their own speed. When they had several planks they would bring them in to the carpenter shop where we would measure each board and pay according to the number of cubic centimeters it contained. The boards would be at least twelve feet long and were seldom completely straight, so they would be turned over to the carpenter who would plane them down until we had some fairly decent lumber. Almost all the boards were fine hardwood, preferred because of its resistance to termites, who did have their limitations. The carpenter went through several plane blades a year.

The lumber was used for doors and door and window frames and to make improvements in the dormitories, which were in deplorable condition. We paved the floor in one building with bricks we had made, put new mats on the ceilings and started making more comfortable beds to replace the planks the boys had been sleeping on. We found that they had no place to keep their clothing and personal effects so we had the carpenter make them some shelves and other simple furniture.

Before I became director I had not paid any attention to the dining hall because it was not my responsibility but one day, out of curiosity, I went to see what it was like. I found that the boys were in the habit of leaving it in a filthy condition with rice all over the tables and the floor. Dirty dishes were left on the tables to be gathered up later by a student who washed them in cold water. Finding that a very unsanitary and dangerous condition, I ordered that two fifty-gallon drums be filled with hot water, one with soap and the other with clear water for rinsing. From then on each student was required to wash and rinse his own plate and spoon. Each afternoon the tables were taken out, the floor swept and the tables scrubbed with hot water and soap, using stiff brushes. The dining hall then had an air of cleanliness we could be proud of. I could not understand how such a state of affairs could exist, and we could see that there was still a lot to do to improve the living conditions of the students.

Meanwhile, Jackie had taken over as church pianist and choir director since she was the best trained musician available. She also organized a choir made up of students from the monitors school. In church every Sunday morning the congregation would drone through English and American hymns translated into Otetela by missionaries without any collaboration with the local people. It was the same as we had seen in Lodja. It was obvious that neither the words nor the music had any meaning for the people and were hardly a suitable vehicle for the expression of true sentiments.

Jackie thought, correctly, that their church music should be more like that of the American Negroes, as they were known at that time. She had had the foresight to go to a music store back home that catered to black people and buy several records we were told contained popular gospel music. We played one of them for some of our teachers, hoping that they would relate more favorably to that than to music that was completely foreign to them. Their reaction was most negative! They were horrified and very angry and would not believe that such music was used in Negro churches in the United States. We were stupefied and could not understand until someone explained that the form of the music, and especially the high female falsetto voice, was exactly the same form used by the witch doctors when they were trying to cure someone who was ill or to perform an act of divination. We then realized that the music they were rejecting was closer to what they would have had if their natural creativity had not been so completely stifled by the missionaries, but because of the indigenous use of that form of that musical form it could not possibly be used in a Christian church in central Congo.

Incidentally, we played the records on a hand-crank portable phonograph like the ones people used to take on picnics in the 1920s. Many of them had been sent to the mission and then given to one of the teachers along with recorded hymns. One of the missionaries expressed concern that if we were not careful the faithful might use the machines to play "jumpy music" and that bothered her.

As the fellow in the fable about Robert Bruce said, "If at first you don't succeed, try, try again." Jackie continued to work with the choir and quietly introduced a Negro spiritual of a more commercial nature titled "I'm a Trampin" after it had been translated into Otetela by the only teacher who spoke any English. It was a great success, and Jackie said that it made chills run up and down her spine. It was from a book on spirituals she had asked someone at home to send to her, so she had plenty of material.

From then on she continued to introduce music that allowed the choir to make use of the natural love of the students and the congregation for rhythm and syncopation. She always made sure the teachers and the students found the music acceptable before she would ask them to perform it in church. Not all the missionaries appeared to share the enthusiasm of the Africans but no one openly expressed disapproval of the new trend.

We only had two African teachers in the monitors school, but they were both very good and one had graduated from the preparatory high school on the Presbyterian mission. Luhahi taught math and science and the other, Kasongo, taught French and several other subjects in the seventh year of the primary school and was in charge of the afternoon activities, the dining hall, and the crew of laborers we kept on to perform necessary tasks like building houses and general housekeeping. They were, we thought, absolutely indispensable to the operation of the school, not only for the teaching they did but for dealing directly with the students and providing continuity.

One afternoon I came home visibly depressed and Jackie asked me what had happened. I replied, "The school has been struck by a catastrophe."

"What do you mean?" she asked. Sadly, I told her that I had been told that Kasongo had been fired. Naturally, she wanted to know why. I explained that someone had found out that he had been paying unauthorized social visits to the wives of the married students while their husbands were engaged elsewhere. I was furious that no one had had the courtesy to inform me of the allegation. I was never told who the informer was or what proof he or she had. All I was told was that the missionaries who had little or nothing to do with the school had insisted that Kasongo, who was loved and admired by all the students, would have to be dismissed because of his alleged dereliction. We had to accept their decision.

To me it was devastating because it meant that although I had quite enough to do I would now have to take on another French class and spend much more time supervising our workmen and doing other things that Kasongo had done. There had been no complaints to me from any of the married students about what would be called now sexual harassment and there probably never would have been because the Batetela had a very different way of looking at such relationships than the missionaries did. I had not done any deep research on the subject but it appeared that sexual misconduct between consenting partners was not considered a capital offense.

The other courses he taught were taken on by other teachers and some of the senior students took over some of his supervisory functions. What I really did not like was payday. There was a system of family allocations, a device used in Belgium to encourage large families, which meant that a man was paid not only his wages for each day he worked but an additional amount for his wife and each child. The school clerk kept track of how many days each man worked, which varied from month to month because most of the men felt there were other things in life besides work, and the number of children varied. I did not have a calculator so I had to spend hours figuring out how much each worker was to receive. It was a tedious and annoying task.

If I had found out about Kasongo I would have expressed shock and disbelief and would have explained why it was important that he did not do anything like that again. I could have suggested to his critics that he undergo a period of counseling with a professional counselor but considering how the missionaries felt about sex the idea would not have received serious consideration. Whoever it was that caused the scandal had no understanding of how important he was to the school, and of course no mention was made of a replacement. But rules were rules and he had to go. He did not suffer at all because he immediately found a position that paid much more than he had been paid as a teacher.

The agriculture program was doing well under the guidance of the first professional agriculturist the school had ever had. The students had a model garden they all worked in one afternoon a week, experimenting with various crops and new ideas, learning things they could later pass on to their pupils. Coconuts were not indigenous to the region but someone had planted a few coconut palms and Fernand was raising coconut seedlings to distribute to the villages. We also had various citrus trees and a few avocado trees. They were not native and were different from the oranges, lemons and grapefruit we were used to. The grapefruit, for example, was what is called a pamplemousse. It had a thick skin, was sweeter than American grapefruit and easier to eat because the fruit inside was divided into sections that came apart easily.

Efforts to encourage the local people to plant fruit trees so they could have plenty of fresh fruit failed miserably, but it was not that they did not like the fruit; they regularly came into our garden to help themselves. They just had a different attitude toward such things as fruit trees than we do. Since no one planted fruit trees they could not belong to anyone and were seen as wild. Therefore, anyone who wanted it could take the fruit and enjoy it. We did not mind their taking the fruit from the trees in our yard as long as they left us enough for our own use, and they always did. After all, we did not plant the trees either. The avocado tree was an exception. It was the only one we had and it grew next to the shed where the laundry was done. We finally learned to listen for the avocados falling on the metal roof of the shed so that we could go out and get them before anyone else did.

We had a hard time understanding why the people did not want to improve their diet by planting trees and raising animals and poultry efficiently. There were reasons, of course, for doing what they did. The idea of planting a tree that would take several years to produce was out of the question and planting something for future generations just was not done. We were even told of one man who had planted a fruit tree and when he moved to another village he cut it down before he left. The French had an expression, *"Le noir est peu prévoyant,"* which means "The African does not have much foresight." It was generally true but on the other hand it may have an advantage. Those who do not look into the future do not worry about things that have not happened.

That part of Africa was sparsely populated, so conservation was not a concern as whole villages could move to a different location if necessary. Another thing that inhibited development and explained the general indifference was the system of land tenure. All the land belonged to the tribe in common and each year the village chief would parcel out the plots of land to the various families, so that each one usually had a different piece of land at least every few years. There was no incentive to develop or improve anything. Besides, all a family needed was enough space to raise rice, millet, and whatever else they wanted to feed the family for a year. Apparently they did plant bananas and papayas because they produce fruit within a short time.

It was depressing to see children with big potbellies resulting from malnutrition that could have been prevented by an improvement in the diet, but there was nothing we could do about it aside from what we were doing. Meat was in very short supply because of the sterility of the soil, which limited the amount of wild game, and the raising of poultry and livestock was not very efficient. There were a few sheep and hordes of goats, which were a real nuisance because they were not penned up and were everywhere looking for food. Moreover, the goats were rarely used for food because they were mainly kept to exchange for wives.

Toward the end of the second year someone suggested that we raise rabbits. It was a very practical idea because they mostly ate greens such as banana and sweet potato leaves, both of which were abundant and free. We built some hutches with chicken wire over a wooden frame and put long legs on them so they were raised off the ground. We soon had all the rabbit meat we wanted and it reminded us of the boarding house in Brussels where rabbit was always the main course on Sunday. Americans do not eat much rabbit but in Europe it is very common. We supplemented the rabbits's leafy diet with rice and millet bran from the school kitchen, as we did with the chickens, and gave them the same mineral supplement. The only losers were the goats who foraged every day at the school kitchen. Raising rabbits was so simple we tried very hard to interest the natives in it because it would have furnished then m with a regular supply of meat with very little effort. We were disappointed that only very few of the teachers even tried.

Another project we had nothing to do with had about the same level of success: the government effort to promote the raising of fish. It was easy to dam up a small stream and stock the pond with tilapia, a fresh water fish that would thrive on the bran thrown out every day. The Belgian administrators would encourage the people to build a pond and provide the fish to get the project started, but unless they followed up the ponds were often neglected and it is doubtful that many survived independence. We had a stream flowing from a spring near our house that would have been ideal for such a project but we never got around to it. There was already a good pond, free of leeches, and that was where the boys went to swim.

The pond was convenient but for real swimming we went to Lake Makamba, several hours from Wembo Nyama, where there were several cottages. We went there once or twice a year on vacation. It was a very restful place because there was no one living near the lake and there were no boats so we had the lake all to ourselves. We were told that the natives thought the lake was haunted and avoided the area completely. The water was fairly warm and there were no leeches, so it was a great place to swim. Each time we went we had to take along enough food, kerosene, and other supplies to last as long as we were there. Sometimes we took our cook and sometimes we did not, depending upon how we felt. The cottages were not entirely finished so each time we went we would find out what needed to be done and make our contribution.

We liked to visit the other mission stations and to see our friends there. Minga was interesting because we had a leper colony there. It was government policy to round up all the lepers and send them to one of the many leper colonies for treatment, colonies that had been so effective that leprosy was rapidly disappearing and it was almost impossible to find anyone with the disease. Unfortunately, as leprosy was being defeated there was an increase in the number of tuberculosis patients so the two nurses in the leper colony had a new challenge. I had great respect for the nurses because they had been there a long time and had devoted their lives to their work.

To reach Minga we had to cross the Lubefu River, a river with a very swift current that made a cable ferry practical. One time we had a frightening experience. The ferry was attached to a cable stretched across the river so that the ferryman could use the current to propel the ferry across the river by moving the rudder. When we reached the river we found that the cable had broken or something and the ferry had been swept downstream, but instead of continuing all the way to Léopoldville it had gone aground after drifting for a mile or so. We had to leave our car on our side of the river and cross in a large, dangerously overloaded dugout canoe with the water not more than two inches from the gunwale. It was a matter of some concern since Jackie did not know how to swim, but we had no choice, and the river was not very wide so we made it safely to the other side.

Someone was there on the other side to take us to Minga and when we returned the next day repairs had been made and we were able to cross on the ferry, a more comfortable means than the dugout canoe. We had mixed feelings about the ferries. Sometimes it was enjoyable but there was often an element of uncertainty and we did not always have the confidence we should have had. Sometimes there were amusing incidents and sometimes it was annoying. One day we arrived at a river with a fairly large ferry at the same time as a large truck loaded with sacks of rice. The captain of the ferry told the driver that it would be dangerous to carry anything that heavy and that he would have to reduce the load on his truck. The driver drove his truck onto the ferry and proceeded to unload his truck, carefully piling the sacks of rice alongside his truck on the ferry. The captain was satisfied so we drove onto the ferry and crossed the river. On the other side the driver reloaded his truck and went on his way.

The ferry on the road to Lusambo was one of the most advanced, technologically. It had an engine, but when the boatman was tired of working he would short out the battery with a wrench so he would not be able to start the engine. He would apologize, saying that the engine would not start. One evening we arrived at the crossing in a driving rain and absolutely had to get to the other side because there was no place to spend the night on our side. We drove onto the ferry, along with several other travelers. Someone then took the battery out of his automobile, put in the ferry engine, started the engine and we were able to cross. On the other side the battery was removed from the ferry, put back in the car and we went on to Lusambo and the welcome comfort of the guest house of the Scottish mission there.

There were very few bridges in the area where we lived because most of the rivers were too wide for bridges. One day we did come to a small stream with a bridge so rickety and unstable in appearance that everyone but the driver got out of the car and went across on foot so the driver was the only one in danger. The crossing was made slowly and gingerly because we had no other way to get to our destination without great inconvenience. The roads in our area were surprisingly good. They were all only one lane, which was enough because there was so little traffic, and they were usually passable except immediately after a hard rain. Each village along the road was responsible for the maintenance of a certain stretch of road and as soon as the rain stopped a crew would come out and make the necessary repairs. The crews were paid by the government and seemed to take much pride in their work, which they did without supervision. There was even one stretch paved with black anthills and we liked that because we could go fifty miles an hour for a few minutes. Automobiles were rare and more than once as we approached an African on a bicycle he would panic and go off into the ditch.

Halfway through the second year our doctor had to go back to Finland. We really missed him and his family; his two boys were just a little younger than our boys and they played together wonderfully well. When they left we bought their short-wave radio and had something new to play with. We used a car battery that had to be recharged periodically for power and really enjoyed listening to the BBC. We depended on Alistair Cooke's regular broadcasts for news about the United States because he was such a good reporter. Our information about what was going on in the rest of the world all came from European or British sources so our understanding of world events was colored by what we heard. For example, during the Suez crisis of 1956, when the British and French were trying to take over the canal we could not understand the attitude of the United States government because we had the impression that the British and the French were justified in what they were doing. We were well settled in by the end of the second year and could see some of the advantages of living in such a place. There were no traffic lights, no traffic, no telephones, no snow, and no television. The boys spent most of

135

their time doing interesting and constructive things like gardening, poultry raising, swimming, and exploring in the forest. The gardener was a real wizard and had transformed a large patch of weeds into a beautiful vegetable garden that produced an adequate supply of vegetables without the use of pesticides. We planted forty coffee trees at the far end of the garden but we left before they were mature enough to bear fruit. We hoped that someone would benefit from them later on.

Jackie was teaching the little children to sing French children's songs like *Quand trois poules s'en vont aux champs,* which is sung to the tune of "Twinkle Twinkle Little Star," as an introduction followed by some serious instruction in music. It was the first time they had a real musician for a teacher and they were very pleased. The choir continued to develop and the quality of the music in church was improving steadily. I had always wanted to learn to play the guitar and had brought one with me, but after years of study all I could play all the way through was "Birmingham Jail," a classic of traditional country music I had learned while I was in the army. I finally realized that I had no talent at all for music so I did the right thing. I gave the guitar to one of the students with the understanding that he was to share it with the others. They did not need any instruction and many of the students became good guitar players. In one year the instrument looked as though it was 100 years old.

Soon after we lost Kasongo another couple from the United States joined the faculty of the monitors school to teach math and science. They were a welcome addition and for once we had almost enough people to run the school properly and had reason for optimism.

Since one of the other boys had pigeons Hari decided that he should have some too, so we built a dovecote and placed it on the top of a pole about eight feet high. He got some pigeons somewhere and they started raising a family. Everything was fine until a dominant male invaded from the other boy's pigeon house and killed Hari's daddy pigeon. With appropriate ceremony the dead pigeon was buried at the lower end of the garden. I noticed that as Hari dug the grave he set up the same sort of rhythmic chant the natives used when doing manual labor. He went on raising pigeons and managed to resolve his dispute with the other boy and get him to agree to keep his pigeons at home.

I had not been at all sure of just what I should be teaching in the art classes at the beginning, and after having taught them something about colors I did not know what to do next. Then one day I was looking at the drab brick walls of the classrooms I remembered the designs I had seen on the walls of some native houses. I asked the students if they would like to decorate the classrooms with decorative borders around the windows and doors. They agreed that it might be an interesting project. I pointed out that we had no paint and no brushes but they said that would be no problem. They explained that they knew how to make brushes out of palm branches and since the only colors we needed were black a white we could use kaolin for the white and grind up charcoal for the black. One of the boys knew where there was a deposit of kaolin so I selected three students to help. We drove about six kilometers to the site, filled a large tub with clay, hauled it up the hill, loaded it into the trunk of the car and came home. For the black we ground up some charcoal and using manioc for the binder, made our own paint. We then proceeded to spend a few hours each week brightening up the classrooms. As usual, I was really impressed with their knowledge of their environment and their ability to make good use of so many things from nature. If they needed rubber for something they knew where to find a rubber tree. The ability to furnish everything they needed to live by using what was available explained, in part, their reluctance to work any more than they had to.

I did my best not to influence the boys in their choice of decoration because I wanted it to be theirs and not mine. The results exceeded my expectations. They were similar to the designs I had seen on a house but adapted to the space being decorated with good taste and a sense of design and proportion. I began to feel that the arts and crafts program was successful. Clay was abundant so the next project was an introduction to ceramics. I did not expect the students to show much interest in it but went ahead as we shall see later.

CHAPTER 10

How I become known as a great hunter without really trying. I become director of the monitors' school. We take a trip to the Katanga.

EVEN THOUGH WE HAD our chickens and rabbits we still liked to have some real red meat from time to time. Occasionally we would get some beef from Lodja, which we would keep in the small freezer of our kerosene refrigerator and enjoy steaks and roasts until it ran out. What other fresh meat we had we bought from hunters who would bring in all types of wild game, but we only bought it after Papa Shuku had examined it and declared it fit for our use. Even so, much of the meat was what we called "gamey" and was only edible after a substantial application of barbecue sauce.

One day a fortunate event occurred. There was one large antelope, called a horse antelope, whose meat was particularly delicious. It was classified as an endangered species and was thus off limits, so even if we had been hunters we could not have shot them. The territorial agent, our local Bula Matadi, was a compassionate man who hated to see animals suffer. Once in a while he would find an animal that had been wounded or injured and if he did it was his duty to put it out of its misery. On the day in question he had found an injured horse antelope he had to dispatch. So the meat would not go to waste, he delivered half the carcass to the Catholic mission at Tshombe Sainte Marie and the other half to us, emphasizing that killing the animal had been an act of mercy. The meat was divided equally and was enjoyed by everyone at Wembo Nyama.

People outside of Africa have been led to believe that all of Africa is teeming with wild game, because that is what they have read and seen in motion pictures and television. It is true that Kenya, Tanzania, and much of southern Africa do have many wild animals because of the favorable climate and the vast game preserves, but there are no more wild animals in most of Africa than there are in the United States; it is just that some are bigger and more exotic and there is more variety. The central Congo was rather poor in wildlife. All the time we were there we never saw an elephant, a giraffe, a hippopotamus, or a lion, although we were told that such animals did exist sixty miles to the east. We just never had the time or the curiosity to go to see if it was true. We knew there were leopards and wildcats because they kept taking our chickens, but we never saw them.

I have never been enthusiastic about hunting, because I do not enjoy killing animals or birds and it always seemed that it entailed some unpleasant aspects, such as getting up very early, carrying lots of equipment, and walking great distances in bad weather. That others do it does not bother me. I did, however, earn a reputation as a great hunter by accident. Almost everyone who goes to Africa feels he must become a hunter, so everyone had a rifle or shotgun or both, and for a while I had a Winchester .30-30 carbine, something I had always wanted since I was a child because it was what the cowboys in the movies carried. I bought it from a colleague who had received it as a gift from one of his supporters.

There was not much to do in the way of entertainment, so from time to time some of the missionaries and Africans would go into the forest to hunt. They never seemed to come back with any trophies of the hunt but they did get a lot of exercise. One day they asked me to go with them. It seemed like a good idea so I got my rifle and we set off. We walked for an hour or two along a path in the dank, humid forest in a strange silence,

The idea of hunting was attractive but hardly any of us had the time to do much of it. For meat we relied upon local hunters, who had more time and for whom it was profitable.

Drumming and dancing were not encouraged by the missionaries.

as though all the creatures living there had been warned of our presence and were being quiet to avoid detection. We did not see anything to shoot at so we turned around and started back.

On the way we saw a bird about the size of a parrot sitting in the top of a tree about 75 or 100 yards away. Most of the people had high-powered hunting rifles suitable for shooting elephants, so they viewed my Winchester with some contempt. One of them asked me if I thought I could hit that bird and I replied that I did not think so. He urged me to try so I raised my rifle, took aim, and fired. To my surprise the bird fell and one of the Africans ran to retrieve it. When he came back he was holding the head in one hand and the body in the other. As a reward he was allowed to keep the bird. It was either a simple case of fantastic luck or all those hours I spent on the YMCA rifle range as a boy had finally paid off. My feat was all the more impressive because my rifle did not have a telescopic sight and word got around that Uwandji Fundji was a crack shot. Some time later I was out with a small group walking through manioc fields looking for guinea hens, a bird about the size of a small turkey and absolutely delicious. All the others had shotguns, because a serious hunter does not hunt birds with a rifle, so I was again the object of some playful derision, but I did not mind; I was just out for the exercise. We had gone quite a distance without seeing any game when suddenly I spotted a plump guinea hen off to my left. I raised my rifle and fired. When we went to pick it up we saw that it had been shot through the backbone and none of the meat had been spoiled. I was the only one who had been lucky so my reputation as a hunter was enhanced. The whole party, including the Africans, came to our house for dinner that evening and we all had a wonderful time. After that I did no more hunting and kept my reputation intact.

The authorities realized that since the country was not overrun with wild game limits had to be put on hunting.

Anyone who wanted to shoot an elephant had to buy an expensive license and if he did shoot one the ivory belonged to the king, but the hunter was allowed to purchase it. There was also a limit on the weight of any piece of ivory that was exported, so people who had purchased a tusk that was delicately carved from one end to the other had to saw it up into small segments and the glue them back together later. As with the horse antelope some species were protected and it was easy to see why. The concept of conservation of wildlife was not understood by the indigenous population, so the possession of modern rifles was restricted to those who were not liable to abuse the privilege. African hunters were allowed to own and to use muzzle-loading rifles, which were beautifully made in Belgium, inexpensive, and rather dangerous if too much powder was used. I have always regretted not buying one for a souvenir.

Meanwhile at the school we began to notice that the students were showing an interest in selecting names to go along with their new status as évolués, a term applied to Congolese who had received more than an elementary education and consequently an ability to adapt to a European lifestyle. Family names did not exist although some names had a prefix meaning "son of," such as On'Usamba, which meant son of Usamba. The students felt that they, like Europeans, should have more than one name so they invented names for themselves, like movie stars, names that seemed amusing to us in some cases but did convey the impression that the bearer of that name was a "somebody."

For example, there was Umo Losombe Emile Cadet Thédore, a very serious, scholarly young man, and Lushima Marcus Tallimard. Many of them found names in the historical section of the Larousse, names like Dagobert, Philibert, or other forgotten kings, dukes, and heroes of the Middle Ages, names that had not been in vogue for centuries. The people of that time must have had a good sense of humor. Charlemagne's mother, the wife of Pépin le bref (Pépin the short), was called Berthe au grand pied (Big foot Bertha).

The students were also refreshingly creative in their use of French and inventing terms that would be unknown in Europe. One such term that originated at the monitors school was *imbécile diplomé,* which means idiot with a diploma, or "certified fool."

At Christmas time there were lots of festivities, beginning with a play in the church, organized and presented by the students without the assistance of any of the missionaries. It was a dramatization of the Christmas story from the Annunciation to the Flight into Egypt, beautifully told with feeling and a certain amount of gusto. The boys were natural actors and not at all inhibited by the audience. The plays were in Otetela and the boys did not need a script; all they needed was an idea of what the story was about, which was easy because they had heard them many times. There were some amusing aspects and the audience laughed more than is customary at a religious play.

There were some scenes that would not have been considered appropriate in a Methodist church in the United States, but they seemed perfectly normal to the audience. For example, where we would have the actors in costumes suggesting biblical times, all the actors wore shoes and some wore long trousers because it was a special occasion and such things had a symbolic significance to them that was understandable but seemed out of place to us. The guards at Herod's court carried long muskets and were dressed like the Congo police in blue denim shirts and shorts, boots, and a red fez. Where they found the costumes and props was a mystery but it showed they had spent much time in preparation.

The choice of events and scenes to be emphasized was interesting. The most important scene was the collection of taxes in Bethlehem, which went on for quite a while with emphasis on the cruelty and arrogance of the tax collectors. They also presented the story of the prodigal son, which had nothing to do with the Christmas story but offered an opportunity for some wild dramatic development. The students had a talent for selecting the scenes that would have the best potential for drama and satire. In the story of the prodigal son most of the action took place while the son was wasting his substance in riotous living. They really enjoyed putting on the barroom scene and it certainly delighted the audience. The plays were all in Otetela and some of the humor may have been a bit vulgar, but I had no way of knowing because my knowledge of the language was so limited.

In January 1955 we received word that the bishop had appointed me director of the monitors school to replace the single woman who had been running the school and was going on furlough. When I took over I found that the former director was no more addicted to administration than I was and had left pretty much of a mess. She had no filing system and we had to spend a lot of time getting things organized. Working with the school clerk, who was very conscientious but had never been given any authority, we soon solved the problem. Administrative work was a bother because it kept me from doing important things like painting and making pottery. No one should be put in a position of responsibility if he is capable of doing anything else.

It was particularly irksome when a student got into trouble and we had to have a special faculty meeting and listen to endless accusations, explanations and excuses. In the process I discovered that I had no lust for power and was not thrilled by being able to tell others what to do. Since everyone on our faculty was responsible, we were able to get by with a minimum of bureaucratic meddling.

We received a fair number of requests for information

about former students, so I dictated a collection of letters in French that the clerk could use as form letters to type in response to most of them. Many were from business people who were looking for reliable help because our graduates, although few in number, were highly regarded and because of the prosperity of the country the need for educated Congolese was outstripping the supply. Other letters concerned falsified documents. We had a high attrition rate so there were many young men out there who had spent one or two or maybe three years in the monitors school but had not graduated. The practice of altering documents was widespread and many of those who had dropped out would use a forged diploma to enhance their job prospects. Many of the requests were from employers who would want to verify a diploma. We always answered the letters but it was a nuisance.

Being Americans, some of us naturally began to consider ways to improve and expand the school. Every year we had to turn away large numbers of qualified students who really wanted to improve their lives through education. Looking to the future and also considering improvements needed for the present I drew up plans for an additional classroom and more suitable dormitories to upgrade the school to what it should be. I showed the plans to our engineer and he agreed that the buildings would not be difficult to build when the time came. Then one day my enthusiasm was dampened when I realized that my plans were all pipe dreams because we would never have enough personnel to carry out any plans to expand the school plant beyond what we had. Supervising any construction beyond what was absolutely essential to maintain what we had was out of the question because I no longer had the time and I had no one to whom I could delegate such a task. Consequently, I let go most of the workers we had.

We had added a fine building for the arts and had a good carpenter with several apprentices so we were able to make furniture for the school and for anyone who needed it. We found that we were able to buy some lumber from a sawmill not too far away that was being run as a commercial enterprise. It was beautiful hardwood and made our work easier because it was all planed and ready to use, so the carpenter no longer had to spend so much time planing down the rough lumber we had been using. Since we did not have a proper place to hang our clothes I had the carpenter build us an armoire. It had legs about a foot long so we could clean under it and destroy any termites that showed up and the doors were made very light by attaching woven mats to a wooden frame. We also made a coffee table and other furniture for the new doctor.

In April 1955 we took a long vacation. First we went to the lake for a few days, then went on to Luluabourg. From there we took a train to the Katanga at the southern end of the country to visit some friends who lived in Mulungwishi. The trip took two nights and a day and the train was not at all what we had expected. We had a second class compartment with private bath just as we would have had at home but it was much cheaper. The only white man on the crew was the dining car steward. All the others, the engineer, brakeman, and so on were Congolese. Paul was really excited about the trip and kept waking us up during the night to ask questions. Because the train did not stop at Mulungwishi we got off at Jadotville, forty kilometers away, and some of our friends came to pick us up. Our stay there was very pleasant and instructive. It was like being in a different world. Our friends lived in a brick house on a tree-lined street that was actually paved. They had electricity twenty-four hours a day, a telephone, shops, and all sorts of things we were beginning to miss in Ewangu. The whole atmosphere was different and that may have been due to the origin of the two missions. Around the time of the Civil War, and I do not know the exact date, the Methodist Church split in two. There was little or no communication between the northern and southern branches for almost 100 years, but they finally did get back together. Meanwhile, the mission in central Congo had been founded by the southern Methodist Church and tended to be very conservative. The mission in the Katanga was the work of the northern Methodists and was much more liberal in its outlook. The Katanga was an industrial region with rich copper mines and other minerals such as diamonds, cobalt, gold, and uranium, which provided a much stronger economic base upon which to build a church. It was also possible to raise temperate climate crops and there were no tsetse flies so stock raising also flourished. Elisabethville, the largest city in the region, was 5,000 feet above sea level and the other cities in the region were nearly that high so the oppressive heat and humidity of central Congo were absent.

We enjoyed visiting the Katanga, but living there would have been like living in Europe and we would have missed out on the exotic and challenging elements that made central Congo different. It was in Jadotville that I found a store that sold silk screen supplies and decided that it would be interesting to teach some of the students to do silk screen printing. When it was time to leave we took the train back to Luluabourg and the drove home.

During another vacation we drove to a lake halfway between Luluabourg and the Katanga, a lake much larger than the one near Ewangu, where the bishop had a cottage. It was in open country with a few trees and quite a few other houses around the lake and on the other side of the lake was a restaurant run by a Belgian family. One evening we decided to take advantage of the opportunity to have a real European meal. We arrived at the restaurant about seven o'clock and had to wait quite a while to be served. By the time our dinner did arrive it was almost nine o'clock and little Paul was so sleepy that he collapsed right into his food. We had forgotten that Belgians did not ordinarily take their children with then when they went out to dinner and their dinner hour was usually later than ours.

We regretted not being able to travel more. The Kivu, in the northeastern corner of the Congo was supposed to be the most spectacular region with a range of high mountains and dense forests that were home to gorillas, but we never had a reason to go there. We did not even manage to visit Tunda, the easternmost of the Methodist mission stations near the Lomami River in a region called the Manyema. That region was the subject of a book titled *Manyema, Pays des mangeurs d'hommes,* which means Manyema, Land of the Man-eaters. We just did not have the time to do much traveling because we were so busy most of the time and I seemed to spend a good part of the short vacations recovering from attacks of malaria.

I had had no occasion to take an interest in automobile mechanics since high school, when I had a 1931 Pontiac I could repair because it was so simple. Our 1952 Chevrolet was more complicated but not too much so and I became fairly proficient at solving problems as they arose. I learned to do simple things like cleaning out the carburetor and the fuel pump. At first it was all a mystery but once Fernand and I learned to fix something we found that it was usually fairly easy. One day when Fernand tried to start the car to go to Usumba, the commercial center, to buy some machetes it would not start. Observing that the glass bulb installed on the fuel line to trap sand was empty we concluded there must be something wrong with the fuel pump. Consulting the service manual, we looked up fuel pumps, read all about how to remove them, take them apart, and repair them. We followed the instructions removed the fuel pump, and finding nothing wrong with it, put it back on the engine. The car started and was running perfectly. We decided that it had not run before because the sediment bulb was a little loose, allowing air to leak in and destroy the action of the fuel pump. All the work we did was unnecessary but we were very proud of ourselves for learning how to operate on a fuel pump. More important, the experience gave us the confidence to tackle other problems. The roads responsible for the steady source of broken springs that furnished fine steel raw material for the blacksmiths were equally hard on shock absorbers, so ours wore out much sooner than they would have on smooth, paved streets. I ordered some new ones and by following the instructions was able to replace them. Then the brakes were acting strangely and attending to them was beyond my ability, so when a young man presented himself saying he was a mechanic I asked him if he knew how to adjust brakes. He assured me that he could so I gave him the keys and told him to go ahead. He was expressly told not to leave the mission compound and he promised not to.

Unfortunately, he did not keep his word and drove into Usumba to show off. To drain the water off the street that ran through the village during the frequent torrential rains there were trenches about four feet wide that sloped down and away from each side of the road. As the mechanic was driving down the main street at an excessive rate of speed he lost control of the car, headed down one of the ditches and neatly flipped the car over on its top. No one was injured and the top was caved in a bit but the worst of it was that the windshield was shattered beyond repair. There was no place in the Congo that kept Chevrolet windshields in stock so we had to order one from the factory, which meant a wait of several months. During that time we drove the car without a windshield and when it rained, which was often, we put a tarpaulin over the top and pulled it down in front. To see where we were going we would lift a corner of the tarp to peek out. Fortunately, traffic was no heavier than usual and we had no trouble.

I found a man who had been in the Belgian army during the Second World War and had learned something about body and fender work, so I had him do as much as he could but he did not have the equipment to install the windshield. When it finally arrived I had to take the car to Lodja where there was a Portuguese mechanic who could put it in. I do not know what we would have done without the Portuguese. They were an essential link in the commercial organization of the country, operating small businesses and providing many services in rural areas. They delivered kerosene and gasoline, served as middlemen in the coffee business and did many things that neither Belgians nor Africans could or would do. In other African countries such services were provided by Lebanese or East Asians who were sorely missed when they were forced out after independence.

CHAPTER 11

A conflict between African and American customs.
The problem of keeping teachers.

THERE WERE SOME CULTURAL differences that brought to mind a question I think used to be posed in physics classes: What happens when an irresistible force meets an immovable object? The Batetela had some deeply-rooted cultural patterns that conflicted seriously with accepted procedure in American society in general and the moral principles upheld by the church in particular. One area where there was a significant and very basic difference was the matter of chastity. There is much less difference between the two societies now than there was in 1956, a time when young men and women were supposed to behave themselves and classes in sex education were unknown.

In America girls were supposed to remain virgin until they were married and it is difficult to argue that the custom did not contribute to stable and harmonious family life. The main purpose of marriage among the Batetela was to produce children, so there was a different emphasis and the idea that a girl should remain a virgin until she was married did not occur to them. As soon as a girl was old enough to have children, and that could be in her early teens, she might go to bed with anyone she fancied because evidence that she could bear children was an asset. There was no stigma attached to illegitimate birth, there were no destitute mothers and no orphans because every child had a home in some family.

That conflict led to a serious problem in the school. The mission had its standards, which were quite appropriate in

Illinois or Georgia and the missionaries were certainly right in trying to uphold the standards they believed in wherever they were, but there were grounds for wondering if such expectations were realistic in Sankuru District under the circumstances.

When our students, who were all in their late teens or early twenties, went back to their villages on vacation they were faced with temptations that must have been hard to resist. They had prospects of a brilliant future since they were being educated and were destined to be leaders in the country with corresponding economic advantages. When the boys went home every nubile maiden in the village could be trying to tempt them. The boys being healthy and virile and there being nothing in the local customs to prohibit pre-marital sex, it seems logical to believe there must have been quite a bit of activity that the missionaries and particularly the single ladies would not condone.

One day after the boys had come back from vacation we received a report from one of the village pastors that one of our students had been misbehaving. He had been seen fooling around with one of the girls in the village and the presumption was that he had done something naughty. Some of the missionaries demanded that the boy be expelled from school. This was of course ridiculous, because if we expelled every boy who succumbed to temptation in that way while on vacation we would have no more students and we would have to close the school. I also remembered the case of Kasongo and with the support of the faculty decided to fight.

I refused to agree to the expulsion and insisted that we have some sort of inquiry to determine the guilt or innocence of the student in question. I asked his accusers what the charge was and they replied that he had been guilty of adultery. I asked if he was married and when they replied that he was not I pointed out that only married people can commit adultery, so he was innocent. I then suggested to them that they accuse him of fornication, but the word was so repulsive to them they were put off balance and preferred to resort to euphemisms. I did not like to be so brutal but this was a serious case, with the future of the school at stake. I asked them if anyone had seen the boy doing the thing he was charged with and they had to admit that the pastor in question had not actually witnessed the act he reported.

I told them that according to the American system of justice and presumably of Belgian justice as well, a person was innocent until proven guilty by solid evidence such as a reliable witness. Unless we had an eyewitness or an accusation by one of the participants I could not agree to expelling the student from school. We wrangled for hours but in the end I won, the boy was not expelled from school and no other boy was accused of such a crime. I did not gain any members for the Shaffer Fan Club, but I felt that I had fulfilled by obligation to protect the students and keep as many of them as possible in school because it was my duty as an educator.

I was more interested in seeing that the boys got through school and were a credit to the institution, because they had shown themselves to be diligent, honest, and reliable. Because of the high moral standards and the strict discipline the boys did develop some very positive habits and had established an enviable reputation for the school. I happened to believe those values were more important than their sex life, which I felt was none of our business. While we had certain ideals and goals it was not in our interest to be overly concerned with less important matters having nothing to do with the basic integrity of the individual.

Some of the older missionaries who were better organized and had a more flexible work schedule did find time for such things as safaris. One of the favorite trips—that is what safari means in Swahili—was to what we called the Bambuli country up north in the equatorial forest where there were pygmies and some gorillas. It took two or three weeks altogether, with arrangements for visitors made by a missionary who led the expedition and hired the porters, a cook, and other personnel. It was just like the movies we had seen of African explorers with a long column of bearers carrying the tents, furniture, and all the other supplies on their heads through tall grass and dense jungle. The only thing lacking was weapons to protect them from hostile natives because there was no longer any need. The tourists made much of the trip in kipois, chairs slung from long poles carried by four African bearers just as Dr. David Livingstone had been carried when he was suffering from malaria or other tropical ailments during his explorations.

I really was not interested in hiking through the forest for a couple of weeks but since that was one of the things anyone visiting the Congo was supposed to do I was discussing the possibility with some of my students one day. I said that I would sort of like to see the pygmies and even a gorilla or two but I did not like the idea of doing all that walking. One of the students laughed and said there was no problem. It was possible to drive there in a car. Going to see the pygmies and the gorillas by car was not as romantic as trudging through the forest, and the missionary was only helping to provide a memorable experience the participants could recount to their envious friends for years to come with appropriate embellishments.

Until 1956 change was barely perceptible in central Congo. Our isolation was nearly complete; we hardly ever saw a newspaper and paid little attention to what was going on in the rest of the country, but then the pace of change began to accelerate. Men who had gone to the city were coming back bringing stories of what life was like in the city and creating a feeling of dissatisfaction with the way things were. Those of us who had hopes of improving the monitors school by adding buildings and staff came to understand that it would be impossible. First of all, many of the missionaries did not even believe that teaching Africans beyond what was needed to become a good Christian was a good thing. The Board of Missions in New York and the bishop felt that education was an important part of our mission but without the support of all the expatriate personnel it was obvious that nothing could be done. There were also other mitigating factors.

There was a built-in conflict for which no one was responsible but which affected the ability of the mission to maintain and improve a viable school system. The main purpose of the mission was to build a church, which meant that the training of pastors and the establishment of churches in all the villages had to receive the most attention. Along with the village churches we also had a school in villages where the people wanted one and would support it. In that case the people of the village had to build a school and a house for the teacher as their contribution. We would then provide a teacher who was paid by the mission, which was then reimbursed by the government.

The mission could probably have paid the salaries of the pastors as well, but that would have established a bad precedent and retarded the establishment of a truly indigenous church. The decision to require the congregation to support the church was a wise one and one that took courage. In a society where the women raised all the food and those men who did work earned very little, there was very little cash around to pay for such luxuries as a village preacher, but in the long run it was the best policy. The church could not grow unless it had the voluntary support of its members.

Both the pastors and the teachers were employees of the mission and it seemed fair that they should have the same salary. The teachers in most cases had more formal education and could speak French while most of the pastors could not, but since the pastors' salaries were geared to the local economy it did not seem to them fair to pay the teachers more. Therefore, their salaries were kept at a level where they did not vary much from those of the pastors. Naturally, there was some resentment on the part of the teachers and it was very difficult to keep teachers in the village schools. To make matters worse, the government began to open public schools for the first time, schools which ended the monopoly of the religious missions. The schools were new, in modern buildings with facilities we could not hope to match, and more generously funded than the mission schools. Our teachers could leave the mission and earn a salary that was ten times what the mission could afford to pay for the same work. The increase in the availability of education was good for the children and the country but it created a dilemma for the missions.

The same thing applied to the nurses we had trained. In addition to those who worked in the hospital and the clinics on the mission stations some were operating small village clinics. When the government set up more rural clinics and expanded the hospital system we naturally lost some of our best nurses. Again, what was good for the people hampered our efforts to provide such services in the name of the church. It was foolish to expect the people we had trained to remain with the mission at a subsistence wage when they could be making a decent living doing the same thing for the government.

Those changes were going to require some reflection on how the role of the missions might be changing in the future. There were large rural areas where the people might not be affected by the changes taking place but there were many who would be attracted to the greater opportunities in the cities. Even though they might want to move, such movement was discouraged by the government, which required that anyone moving from his village to the city have a permit and evidence that he had a skill which would enable him to make a living.

That was a wise policy because it prevented the building of shanty towns on the edge of the cities. Anyone who has seen the crime-ridden slums that have grown up in African cities since independence would agree with that policy. For most people in the Congo the traditional life was much more comfortable than life in the city.

The missionaries who had been working among the Batetela for decades had done their work well and had established a little empire in which they were very comfortable. I do not mean that in a derogatory sense, but they did have a situation in which they were in control of what happened and only wanted to work within the framework they understood, immune to outside influences. They spoke the language well and always communicated in Otetela rather than French and could deal with most situations without using French. I did not know how well the older missionaries spoke French because I never heard any of them use it, even with our territorial agent who usually spoke English.

There were times when disputes arose among the people, usually over a woman, when even the most experienced missionaries were baffled by the subtleties of the "palavers" that could go on for days until an agreement was finally reached. Their system of law or custom was every bit as complicated as ours but instead of lawyers they relied on the wisdom and experience of the elders. Even the Belgian administrators deferred to the elders to resolve problems which did not include a real crime but were more in the nature of civil suits governed by local customs.

Since we were outsiders and did not fit in because of differences in background and means of expression our relations with the other Americans varied from very cordial and friendly with some to proper and polite with others. One would think that in such a small community there would be quite a bit of socialization, but during our four years there we were not invited to anyone's home more than two or three times. One reason was, of course, that we had so little time and we spent most of our free time with our children, doing things like reading books and playing cards on Sunday afternoon. We were surprised that playing cards was also considered sinful but we enjoyed it and considered it a wholesome form of family entertainment.

The exception was Thanksgiving Day when we all go together for dinner. We had a sumptuous banquet with all the ladies taking advantage to show off their skill in preparing one of their favorite regional dishes. Every year there was a dispute over which kind of dressing we would have for the turkey. Several regions were represented and each lady believed that her recipe was the best. In the interest of tranquillity I was willing to cooperate and eat anything but to the women it was a matter of great importance.

One reason we got along so well was that we were all so busy doing the things we were supposed to be doing we had no time for mischief. Except for one woman who was a harmless and charming source of gossip, we only had one source of discord, but it seems that there always has to be one. She was the only person who had time to be truly malicious and she worked overtime to fulfill her destiny. Among ourselves we called her Madame Queen, with apologies to Amos and Andy. It was just that she had such a regal manner and seemed to enjoy stirring up trouble. She showed very poor judgment and caused much unnecessary misery on the mission but her husband was such a decent fellow and so useful to the mission no one had the courage to confront her.

Every four years the Methodist Church has what is called a general conference, attended by delegates from the various areas included in a jurisdiction. In this case it was central and southern Africa and included the Congo, the Rhodesias, Angola, and Mozambique. It was time for politically-inclined

Many of the functions of government were left in the hands of the traditional authorities—chiefs and councils of elders—who could solve problems relating to native customs. They were inclined to dress appropriately to show they were important.

One of the missionary wives was concerned about the lack of wholesome recreational activities. She decided to teach the children to play games to keep them out of trouble.

clergy and some laymen to strut their stuff, and there is more political activity and jockeying for power in such organizations than most people who are not involved might realize. There are people who thrive on meetings, listening to speeches and feeling that they are influencing the course of history, but I have always found such proceedings boring. The Africans were allowed to vote for delegates to the general conference that was to take place in Elisabethville in the Katanga because of its convenient location.

I was surprised when it was announced that I had been elected as one of the delegates. I supposed it was because I was perceived as having a more positive attitude toward them than some of the other candidates and the local people thought that I might better represent their interests. Africans have an uncanny ability to understand intuitively how a person feels about them and I had never felt they were inferior as some of the other Americans apparently had.

We drove to Luluabourg where we caught the train for Elisabethville, the same one we had taken to Mulungwishi and we all enjoyed the trip very much. For the Africans' delegates it was the first time some of them had been away from home so they showed a keen interest in things we would have taken for granted. Everything was fine until the porter came to make up the berths for the night. All the missionaries were in one or two compartments and all our Congolese delegation was in another compartment. There was not enough room in the assigned compartments for all the missionaries so one of us was assigned to another compartment which he would have to share with other travelers, including an arabisé, an African from West Africa who had been converted to Islam. There were few such men in the Congo, mostly members of the Fulani tribe, a seminomadic people who occupy a vast area of the Sahel, the territory just south of the Sahara, from Mali to the Sudan. The Fulani were usually tall, very proud, and dignified and many of them were traders, drifting from one country to another without seeming to have to submit to the formalities of passports and visas. When my colleagues found that one of them was assigned to a compartment he would have to share with a strange African they became very upset. Seeing their discomfort and convinced that no harm would come to me, I offered to change places with him and woke up the next morning alive and well.

Elisabethville looked much like Jadotville but I saw very little of it because I had to spend so much time at the conference, something I had not expected to do. I was on only one committee so I did not take part in the important discussions that would influence policy. One thing I did notice was the almost complete absence of trees or other vegetation. In the distance, alongside a huge mound of tailings that resembled a pyramid and a very tall smokestack, suggesting that the barren landscape was due to the pollution from the copper smelters. At that time little thought was given to environmental protection and the pollution was just part of the price to be paid for the creation of vast wealth and good jobs.

The delegates to the conference were an interesting and varied group, with representation from other countries beside the Congo. Because all the countries were colonies peace reigned everywhere and travel between countries was easy. There were many speeches, including one by a visiting American bishop. He spoke in English, naturally, and since most of the Congolese delegates did not understand English someone had to translate what he said. I was assigned as the official translator for the bishop because I had taken my French studies more seriously than most of the others. At least it gave me something to do. Most of the pastors from central Congo did not have even reasonable fluency in French, so after every sentence someone had to translate my French into Otetela. It was cumbersome and humiliating for our delegation. The pastors and other delegates from the Katanga all spoke French and some could also speak English and several African languages, including Kingwana, the local name for Swahili.

The only ones from central Congo who spoke English were two pastors who had been sent to Rhodesia to study in a theological seminary. The preachers in central Congo were working in the villages among people of their own tribe so there was no pressing need for them to learn French. As for the scriptures, they had been translated into Otetela so no other language was required. Too much education for the pastors could have been counterproductive because well educated Congolese tended to succumb to the attractions of the city. I could feel the resentment of the Congolese delegates who were important at home but felt like country bumpkins among the better educated and more sophisticated southerners. The delegates from Rhodesia spoke English fluently and those from Mozambique and Angola spoke Portuguese.

I really felt sorry for the Congolese members of our delegation because for most of them at least it was the first time they had been to a city so there was some culture shock involved. Their inability to speak French, which had become the national language, presented them from communicating with people from other areas. Those from the eastern part of Batetelaland could also speak Kingwana but it was of limited use in most of the country. To get back to the conference, translating for the bishop was not too difficult except when one of the anecdotes he used to illustrate a point in his speech was about baseball. No one in the audience had any idea of what a baseball was so translating the story into French was a real challenge. I had no idea how the Otetela translator handled it.

When the conference was over we all took the train back to Luluabourg and then drove back to Wembo Nyama. The only thing I remember about the business conducted at the conference was that a decision was made to elect an African bishop as soon as possible. That was a victory for the Congolese delegates and an indication that the church was moving in the right direction. The conference suggested a very generous salary for the new bishop, one that was quite unrealistic and there was no explanation of where the money was to come from. They must have resolved that problem because several years later we learned that one of our graduates had become a bishop. I could not help wondering how the members of our delegation were affected by the affluence and the higher level of education of their counterparts in the southern part of the country, but what they had seen must have influenced their thinking and given them a preview of what was to come.

Until this time security had not been a problem. We could go anywhere in the country without fear of being robbed or attacked. Our homes were very vulnerable because not only did we not lock the doors, but the windows only had screens, so anyone who wanted to could enter the house any time he wanted to. Then as more people came back from the cities with reports of what they had seen, attitudes began to change and people began to want things they had not wanted before because they had not known they existed. They were becoming consumers and in anticipation of the increased desire for material things the government tried in a number of ways to encourage industry, such as the raising of cash crops like cotton and coffee. Efforts to increase agricultural production were not as successful as they had been farther south because of the climate and other mitigating factors.

Some did find legitimate ways to increase their income so they could satisfy their new wants, but others resorted to less socially acceptable means. Crimes such as theft and burglary had been insignificant before, but we began to have burglaries in our houses. The robberies usually took place while we were all in church on Sunday morning so we decided that we had to do something about it. Every Sunday morning one of us had to patrol behind the houses with either a rifle or a shotgun, hoping that the mere presence of an armed guard would deter any potential thief. We certainly did not want to shoot anyone and fortunately our plan worked. When our house was robbed the thief took an engraved silver spoon that had been given to us as a souvenir when we left Spearfish. It was not worth much to anyone else but had considerable sentimental value to us. The boy who took it was later caught trying to break into the house next door and was turned over to the Bula Matadi, who searched his house and found the spoon. He kept the spoon, saying he needed it for evidence, and we never did get it back. The boy was not punished because the authorities had never figured out how to punish people for such crimes. Prisons were so comfortable that incarceration was no punishment at all and certainly not a deterrent. Before the arrival of the Europeans a thief would be sold into slavery or to another village where he probably wound up as the main course at the next village banquet. It was harsh but economical and effective. That the colony was going to be developed there was no doubt, but in the process there were going to be many changes, not all of them good, and some of the customs that had made life pleasant would disappear.

CHAPTER 12

Health problems in the equatorial zone. The build-
ing of the new mission hospital.
Rosebud comes to join the family.

AN IMPORTANT CAUSE for the lack of development in the
Kasai was the debilitating diseases flourishing in the heat and
humidity that provided such a hospitable environment for all
types of parasites and bacteria. Some were actual killers and
others merely drained one's vitality and lowered life expec-
tancy. Malaria, sleeping sickness (trypanosomiasis), filariasis,
skin ulcerations, leprosy, and jiggers were all common. Fortunately, we did not have bilharzia, which was endemic in Egypt,
and yaws.

It was sleeping sickness that retarded development of much
of central Africa within ten degrees of the equator by prevent-
ing the use of draft animals, which meant that all farming and
gardening had to be done by hand and much less efficiently. It
was also responsible for the greatest loss of life among the
human population. At first it was confined to Senegal, but at
the turn of the century sleeping sickness began to appear
throughout West Africa and then the rest of the continent. It is
spread by the tsetse fly, which is about the size of a horse fly,
and when it attacks it does so silently so there is no warning. It
thrives in low brush along river banks and is practically impossible to eradicate. The symptoms are fever, swelling of the
lymph glands, and a gradual physical and mental deterioration
that ends in death. There were several victims living near the
mission station who could be seen wandering aimlessly, often
completely naked. They were harmless and well taken care of,

but there was really nothing that could be done except see that they were fed. Most of the Africans must have had an immunity because not many of them suffered from it, but white people had no immunity so we were given pentamidine shots every six months. The shot was administered in the buttocks and hurt for six months until the next shot was given in the other side. Even though we were protected from the disease, if we were bitten by an infected tsetse fly we knew it because the place we were bitten would be red and swollen for a few days. The bites were always on the ankles and usually dated from a time we took a ferry across the river because that was where the flies were the most numerous.

I had one tropical ulcer that started out as a small sore and rapidly grew to a diameter of about an inch. It was bothersome so I went to the doctor. He gave me a shot of penicillin, which cleared up the ulcer, but then I came down with a severe case of urticaria because I was allergic to penicillin and spent a week in bed horribly swollen. We all had malaria in the sense that it was impossible to avoid being infected in spite of such precautions as mosquito nets, screens, and frequent spraying with DDT. The malaria was suppressed by frequent doses of antimalarial drugs such as Aralen, which worked as long as we were in good physical condition. Unfortunately, because of my excessive work load I was usually exhausted by the end of each school term and spent a week in bed with chills and fever, taking increased doses of some drug other than the one I had been taking.

The most troublesome annoyance was the jigger flea, a parasite introduced in 1872 by a British ship from Brazil, which by 1890 had spread through all of Africa. It is not to be confused with the chigger, a common but less deadly nuisance in the southeastern part of the United States. The female jigger burrows under the skin, her favorite place being under the toenails or between the toes. She then lays eggs which grow into a white sac as large as a small pea that begins to itch terribly. If it is not removed in time, the eggs hatch and if they get into the bloodstream the results can de disastrous. To remove them we used a tool made by the local blacksmiths that resembled a three-inch needle that had been flattened out on one end to a width of half an inch. Razor sharp, it was the ideal instrument for removing jiggers.

Removing jiggers was not the sort of thing we would bother the medical personnel with because they had more important things to do, so we soon learned how to do it ourselves. It was very important to remove the sac without breaking it and releasing the eggs. It was under the outer layer of skin so if a small incision was made the egg sac could be removed intact without drawing blood if we were careful. We always wore shoes, usually the tennis shoes that were one of the few items of clothing available in the village shops. Because of the dampness they were more practical than leather but they did not protect us completely from the jiggers.

Filaria was a disease caused by a worm that would get into the bloodstream and travel through the veins and arteries. A person would suspect he had filaria if he felt that something was crawling on his arm but there was nothing to be seen on the surface. We were told that the only way to get the worm out was to watch the patient at night and roll the wire-like worm on a match stick as it crossed the eyeball. I never saw that done and wondered if it was not just a tale to horrify newcomers to the tropics, but the same procedure was described in the case of the guinea worm so it might have been true.

Staying healthy in the tropics requires more attention and can take more time, and more things can happen, so we were fortunate in having a doctor to take care of us. There were times when there would be a hiatus of several months between the departure of one doctor and the arrival of his replacement.

During that interval we still had qualified nurses and our trusty copy of the *Manuel du dispensaire tropical,* a French translation of a treatise on tropical medicine written by a British doctor who described all the common tropical diseases and how to treat them. It was a reliable source of information, written in simple language that anyone could understand. Jackie's course in tropical hygiene at Hartford was also helpful. It was taught by a woman doctor who had spend many years in tropical climates and during the lectures she referred to actual cases she had seen, often ending with the words, "and then she died"—a strange way to inspire confidence but realistic.

After our Swedish doctor left he was replaced by a Hungarian and he was welcomed enthusiastically by the whole community. His specialty was gynecology but he was also a skilled surgeon and neurologist. He had to leave Hungary after the war because he was an aristocrat and had been a medical officer in the Hungarian army and felt that it would not be prudent to fall into the hands of the Russians. He and his wife escaped to Austria and had made an arrangement whereby the Methodist Board of Missions would sponsor him as an immigrant in exchange for two years of service in the Congo. He established cordial relations with the witch doctors of the area, a wise move because they had been known to oppose having their patients treated at the hospital. He also consulted with them and respected their knowledge of medicinal herbs. When he found that none of his medicines were effective against a particular skin rash he asked for advice and found that there was a local remedy that worked. His relations with the witch doctor also helped him build up a respectable collection of fetishes, some of them of very high quality.

The hospital had been built many years before and was quite primitive in some ways but still did a good job of providing excellent medical care. There was a doctor present most of the time, one or two American or Belgian nurses and a well trained local staff of nurses and laboratory technicians, including some whose training went beyond what nurses ordinarily received.

Care could have been free of charge but it had been found that people do not appreciate anything unless they have to pay for it and will often not take the medicine unless it has cost something. The charges were modest: a few francs for medicine or a consultation and fifty francs, about one dollar, for the delivery of a baby, including prenatal care and a layette. Most of the babies were delivered by experienced midwives but the doctor was always available immediately if there were complications. Patients who were confined to the hospital had to bring relatives who camped out behind the hospital and prepared the patient's meals.

Government support of the hospital was extremely generous. All the doctor had to do was submit a list of drugs and supplies to the regional medical officer and all he requested was supplied without question. Considering the number of hospitals and clinics in the Congo, all of which were well staffed, there is no doubt that the Congolese had easier access to medical care than many Americans and no one asked them if they had insurance. In the 1940s a decision was made to build a new, modern hospital to replace the old one. The Board of Missions commissioned an architectural firm to design the building with the understanding that all the Board of Missions would have to pay was the cost of drafting the plans. It must have been a grand design because the cost of the plan was considerable, but the plan by itself was useless. The hospital, as designed, could not possibly have been built with the unskilled labor available at Ewangu.

In anticipation, the Board of Missions sent out someone in the late 1940s to supervise the construction of the hospital. Because of the remoteness of the site he had shipped out the sawmill, the brick making machine, a well drilling rig, a machine for making cement roof tiles, a large diesel generator, and a complete array of power tools. He installed the brick plant, the sawmill and the generator and then built a large building to house all the power tools. Just getting all the equipment there and set up was a great accomplishment, but then he resigned and, as they say, went on to pursue other interests.

The sawmill had a five-foot blade with carbide tips that had to be replaced often because some of the wood was so hard, and there was a vat for soaking the softer woods in a chemical which would deter termites. The new engineer got a permit from the government to cut down enough trees in the forest to furnish the lumber for the hospital and other needs. A crew of men in the forest was able to bring in large logs on the mission truck and saw them into usable lumber. The brick plant produced several thousand bricks a day when it was in operation. It was installed at the base of a hill with a large deposit of clay that made fine bricks. A small bulldozer was used to push the clay down to the machine, doing the work of seventy men working with shovels. When I was told about it I thought of how wonderful it would be not to have to compute the wages of seventy men.

The drilling rig did not appear to have been used although the idea of having a well seemed to be a good idea, and the roof tiles leaked so the project was abandoned. Maintaining all that equipment took up much of the time of the two Americans who were there, the engineer and his assistant who was a very good mechanic and who had been there during the original installation, since there were no Congolese who could be relied upon or had sufficient training. For example, the driver of the bulldozer was given the responsibility of taking care of it but he did not fully understand the machine and neglected to grease it properly. All the gears burned out and had to be replaced after a wait of several months.

Some of the employees, like the driver of the mission truck, were good workers but were limited by their inability to speak French. The engineer asked if one of our graduates or even someone who had dropped out but could speak French well enough to read instruction manuals would be interested in becoming a trained mechanic. Unfortunately, anyone with a high school education felt that he was above any occupation that involved working with his hands. It would have been a good opportunity for a young man to receive valuable training that would have allowed him to make a very good living, but there were no takers and our engineers continued to waste a lot of time doing things a relatively unskilled person could do.

In 1956 the government offered to pay for the construction of a maternity wing as an addition to the existing hospital, using a standard plan that had been successful throughout the country. The offer was accepted and at last something was going to be built that was related to the hospital. The next step was to go to the colonial administration for a hospital plan because the government had built many hospitals in the Congo and had plans that were simple and practical. There were Portuguese and Italian contractors who had the experience and well trained workers who could have built the hospital much sooner and at much less cost, saving the mission both time and money. They probably would have had to live on or near the mission compound during the project, but that would have been unacceptable because first of all they were not American and secondly because the contractor and his assistants might smoke or even drink wine as southern Europeans are apt to do. The missionaries could not risk having the faithful see a white person committing such horrible sins, so they did what my aunt used to call "cutting off your nose to spite your face." It seems absurd now but the people who ran the mission actually were so naïve that they believed they could control every aspect of the lives of the people around them and ignore what was going on in the rest of the world. They were in the vanguard of the movement to guarantee a smoke-free environment and were determined regardless of the cost.

The policy was foolish if not outrageous because the money they were wasting was not theirs to waste. Because of a prejudice shared neither by the Catholics nor the neighboring Presbyterians around Luluabourg, who were also considered to be Christians, every other project was delayed for years because nothing else could be done until the hospital was built. The hospital was finally built, but by that time we had left and we never got to see it. I only saw the inside of the old hospital once, when the doctor had me come in for an X-ray one day when we had electricity.

Before our daughter was born the doctor told Jackie he did not believe in using drugs during childbirth. Instead, he had her follow a régime of exercises so she would be prepared for natural birth. When Martha was born in December 1956 the doctor and the Belgian nurse came to the house and delivered the baby in our own bed. Everything went smoothly; I know because I was there holding Jackie's hand the whole time. That is really a much more civilized way to bring a child into the world, since there is less danger of infection than there is in a hospital. We named the girl Martha but called her Rosebud because the sheets and pillowcases someone had sent us had rosebuds on them.

At the beginning of our third year there were enough missionary children to justify opening a school for them at Minga. Having a more organized education seemed like a good idea because the mothers were constantly being distracted by other obligations that caused them to neglect their children's education. A teacher was sent out who would have no other duties than taking care of the children. Hari seemed to adjust well and it probably was good for him to have a more normal school experience. We were not pleased, however, when we found out later that his teachers had told him his father was in trouble because he had not been "saved." At the same time Paul was old enough for first grade and had regular lessons, but he still had a tendency to slip away as often as he could to play with his African friends. In some ways he almost seemed more African than American.

One day something happened that reminded me of how people working in the Congo were so dependent upon each other in time of need just as they were in the western United States, where towns could be more than fifty miles apart. One afternoon, rather late, the Belgian who ran the butcher shop in Lodja came to the mission and said he needed help. It seemed that a truckload of cattle was overdue and he said he was greatly concerned. Because of the lack of communications he needed to go himself to try to find the truck but he was low on gasoline and while he had enough to get back to Lodja he could not drive very far south without fear of running out. Strangely, no one had any gas to spare but our car had enough in the tank so I offered to drive him to Lubefu or farther if necessary because a truckload of cattle was a terrible thing to lose. After all, we did get meat from Lodja occasionally ourselves.

We drove to Lubefu and by the time we got there it was dark. We found the truck and the cattle were in good condition. Then I noticed I was a little short of gas myself so I went into one of the small shops to see if I could buy some. The man who ran the shop appeared to be an African and spoke French unusually well. Even though he was as dark as the average Mutetela, he said he was Portuguese and had probably come from Angola. He invited us into his home and introduced us to his wife, who had very white skin and was obviously European. He told us she had been sent out from Portugal to marry him, a sort of mailorder bride. Surrounded by small children, they seemed perfectly happy.

The Portuguese, unlike the British, the Americans, and

most Europeans, had little racial prejudice and had no problem with intermarriage with the indigenous populations of Angola and Mozambique. The Portuguese were severely criticized for the way they administered their colonies because they were considered oppressive and showed little interest in such things as education and development, so I was pleased that they did something for which they could be admired. Even though he was not supposed to sell gas retail he sold me enough to make sure I could get back to Wembo Nyama. The man from Lodja was secure in the knowledge his cattle were safe and went home.

Without telephones communication outside the cities was difficult. We had a shortwave radio on each mission station and every day at noon someone would go to the radio shack to exchange information with the other stations. Other mission stations also had their own radio networks and a licensed ham operator as we did. Ham operators send each other postcards after communicating and the collections of cards decorate the radio shacks. I designed a very tasteful card for our ham operator. Sometimes we talked with Hari in Minga, but he seldom had much to say and after a few remarks would say, "That's all I have to say." We also had couriers on bicycles who would carry messages to other stations, some more than 100 miles away. For communicating with the outside world we had MAS, a very reliable means of transport for people as well as cargo and the mail. It probably would have been interesting to travel that way to Lusambo, but it would have put our sanity in question and we never had enough curiosity to do it.

CHAPTER 13

We are invited to a spectacular entertainment
featuring local drummers and dancers. The nature
and purpose of African sculpture.

OCCASIONALLY THE BELGIAN territorial agent would arrange for some entertainment in the form of drumming and dancing, things the local people did extremely well. All the guests would be seated in the shade and groups of men armed with spears and wearing traditional costumes that included a headdress decorated with feathers would act out a battle between rival groups of warriors. The Batetela had been renowned for their prowess and courage and they did look formidable, especially when they would approach us and pretend to attack. After the war dance a sensitive looking young man appeared who played an instrument called a losese. Mounted on a gourd, it resembled a mandolin and had three strings the player plucked to produce the softest, most delicate sounds I had ever heard. Part of the time he sang in a low voice that harmonized perfectly with the instrument and we were sorry we did not have a tape recorder because the music was so beautiful.

Then several dozen women, most of them young with very dignified, erect posture came by doing a typical African dance, shuffling gracefully to the music of the drums.

The group of drummers, most of them using the lukumbi, or talking drum, produced a sound that was truly mesmerizing. After listening for an hour I felt as though I was under a spell and thoroughly relaxed. The rhythms they used were very complicated, with a drummer playing five beats with one hand while the other played thirteen. Batetela drumming moved me more than any other music I heard. Much of the time, and regularly at the time of the full moon when there was some light, we could hear the drumming from the neighboring villages at night when we went to sleep and it was most pleasant. Such activity was not encouraged near the mission because dancing in any form was considered evil, but with no competing sounds such as we have in a city, the sound carried from quite far away. The stars were much bigger and brighter than they are near big cities because they have no competition.

Having studied African sculpture before leaving the Unites States and also in Belgium, I was seriously interested in acquiring as much of it as possible. During one vacation Fernand and I took a short trip or safari, lasting a few days, into the Basonge country to the east and south because the area had a great artistic tradition. Some of their grotesque masks were among the finest examples of African sculpture and their figurines, many of which were hermaphroditic, have a sophisticated charm that is delightful. The Batetela themselves, who were linguistically related to the Bakuba farther south, also a tribe with a great artistic tradition, produced very little sculpture and that was of poor quality.

We toured for several days with only a vague idea of where we were going because we did not have a map of the area, spending the nights in rest houses called gîtes that had been built as places for government administrators to spend the night when touring. We did not find as much sculpture as we had hoped for because Belgian anthropologists and other collectors had been there before, but we did find enough to reward us for the effort. The interesting thing was that after we entered a village and found someone who spoke French so that we could explain what we wanted the people would disperse and come back a short time later with figurines no longer in use that had been discarded. They were delighted to receive a few francs for things they considered absolutely worthless. We found only one mask of a type described in books on African sculpture as a kifwebe as though it was a particular type of mask. The word simply means mask and any Basonge or other tribal mask would be called a kifwebe.

Some Americans and Europeans deplore what they consider the looting of Africa's cultural heritage. According to Emil Torday, a Hungarian explorer and anthropologist who had gone through the Batetela region about 1907 with Hilton-Simpson—who was collecting artifacts for the British Museum—the people had generally ceased to believe in the power of fetishes in the form of anthropomorphic figurines, so that production diminished considerably and interest in their cultural heritage was very slight. The purpose of the fetishes remained but took other forms of expression.

Most Africans were animists who believe that every living thing and every tree and rock has a spirit. All those spirits are potentially dangerous and need to be controlled, and that was one of the functions of the fetishes. A person seeking protection from evil spirits would have a carver make a fetish in the accepted style, a style that could not vary from that established by tradition. A carver who decided to be creative and varied from the tradition would be ostracized. That is why collectors can look at a piece of African sculpture can tell what tribe it represents and the place where it was made. The owner of the fetish would take it to a witch doctor and have some special medicine placed in a cavity in the head or the abdomen. Someone once compared that to having a battery charged. Once it had been charged the spirit lodged in the fetish would protect its owner from harm. I asked my students if the fetishes I had would protect me and they just laughed, saying that until it was "charged" by a witch doctor it was just a piece of wood.

The missionaries, most of whom regrettably were not interested in learning about pagan customs, thought the carvings were idols that were worshipped as gods, and one of the older men proudly told me he had had truckloads of "that junk" burned. I found that depressing. It is a good thing there were Europeans who appreciated the beauty of African tribal sculpture because it was they who saved the masterpieces we can see in European and American museums.

According to Batetela theology there is a supreme being who created the earth, but he is very remote and not interested in the daily activities of creatures on Earth. The people were even afraid to pronounce his name, in the same way the Israelites would not pronounce the name of Jehovah. They also believed no one dies but when he ceases to live his spirit not only continues to live but is always present and can intervene in the lives of the living for good or for evil. Knowing nothing about the true cause of death, they also believed there was no such thing as a natural death from disease. If a person died it was because someone had caused his death by the use of some sort of black magic. In such cases a witch doctor could be called in to find the culprit.

Witch doctors were also useful in the recovery of stolen property. There were cases reported by reliable witnesses involving the identification of a thief who had stolen a bicycle or some other object of value. The witch doctor would perform the required ceremony and then announce that he had put a curse on the thief and if the property was not returned the thief would die or suffer some catastrophe. The property would be returned to its rightful owner because the thief believed in the power of the witch doctor. It was that belief that gave the witch doctor his power. Others who believed that someone had used black magic to put a curse on them actually died from fear with no scientific evidence of an organic illness.

We had an opportunity once to watch a witch doctor in action. We had no idea of why he was doing what he was doing, but the procedure itself was fascinating. The witch doctor was a very dignified person whose very presence inspired confidence. He appeared to have a thorough understanding of psychology and much of his success must have been due to his ability to analyze his patients, discover the problem, and then prescribe a cure. He had a gourd filled with bones, small animal horns, and other objects that he poured out onto the ground and studied. There was musical accompaniment and it was a most impressive spectacle.

Scarification as a means of adornment was practiced throughout Africa, but rarely to the extent found among the Batetela women. The custom was dying out because the missionaries and some of the Africans themselves were not comfortable with partial nudity because it represented a primitive state they were trying to leave behind. Many of the women had their entire torso, front and back, covered with geometric designs. To make the scars an incision was made with a very sharp knife and the resulting wound was filled with ashes so that when it healed it would leave a raised scar. The face was usually left unscarred or had one small scar on each cheek as tribal identification. One of the doctors told me that when he had to perform surgery on women he did his best not to disturb the design. The women also had elaborate coiffures at times that took several days to complete and some of them used a neck rest for sleeping, like the Japanese women, to protect their hair. Some Americans have tried to imitate African hairdressing but I don't think they have ever quite achieved the elegance of the Batetela women.

Even though Batetela women had to work hard it would be an exaggeration to say that they were oppressed. Men had to pay a bride price to the father of the bride and if at any time the woman was dissatisfied she could leave her husband and return home were she would be protected. The bride price would be returned and if the father did not have the funds, having spent the money to buy another wife, for example, it could lead to a difficult situation. One custom that was not fully understood by outsiders was polygamy. Monogamy seemed to work pretty well in Europe and the United States and was recommended by the church, so some of the missionaries tried to impose it on Africans without understanding African culture. They attributed polygamy to lust on the part of the men or the desire of chiefs and wealthy men to show off their power by accumulating wives. That may have been true in some cases but the custom developed and was maintained for other reasons.

Polygamy was basically a sensible means of family planning and it worked very well in that respect. The first, or senior wives were generally pleased to have their husband take an additional and younger wife because the second wife lightened the burden of the first wife by working in the fields, sharing the household chores and taking care of the children. A more important reason was to protect the health of the women. After a woman had given birth she could not have intercourse again for several years, during which she nursed the child and gradually recovered her strength. Each wife had her own house, so her privacy was assured. Where the missionaries were able to impose their will and abolish polygamy the death rate among young women who had children too often went up.

The Batetela were noticeably different from the surrounding tribes and had been so for some time. Early explorers described them as being stronger, more intelligent and more willing to accept innovation than the others. This may seem to contradict what I have said about the reluctance to embrace agricultural innovations; it is just that compared to other tribes in the Kasai they were more progressive. Many of the characteristics that made them stand out were probably the result of their long collaboration with the Arabs. We could not help noticing that many of the people in our area were lighter in color and had features which suggested a racial mixture. They also raised rice, which gave them a better diet than those who subsisted mainly on manioc had.

According to ethnographers who had studied the movement of people in Africa, such as Oskar Baumann and Diedrich Westermann in their great work *Les peuples et les civilisations de l'Afrique,* the Batetela had originally migrated from the north and had driven the Basonge out of some of the territory they occupied. There were differences between the northern and southern sections of the tribe, those who lived mostly on land from which the forest had been cleared and those who still lived in the equatorial forest. The people in the north tended to be more conservative, less advanced, and less affected by foreign influence. To maintain order and preserve tradition the tribe had a secret society called the kum'okunda or lords of the forest. It was their duty to make sure that all the tribal customs were scrupulously respected, and they were more active in the north. They were not chiefs who had administrative responsibilities and we were told that the people did not even know who they were.

I do not remember the details and I had no personal experience with them, fortunately, but we were told they were connected with the "leopard men" who wore claws made of iron just like a leopard's claws and who attacked and killed their victims in such a way that the death could be attributed to a leopard. The victims may have been men who had violated some tribal taboo. I would not have believed the story if I had not seen in the Congo Museum a set of the claws with a description of their use. Such practices were apparently not in use in the area where we lived.

Except for drumming and dancing there did not seem to be much in the way of organized entertainment. The men did raise their own tobacco, which they smoked in a water pipe made from a gourd. When someone told me that one of my workmen smoked hemp I did not know what he was talking about, but I have since learned that it was cannabis, also known as hashish or marijuana. The men also made palm wine and those who could afford it indulged in beer available in the local shops, but I never saw anyone using any of those stimulants to excess. Someone in the colonial administration must have thought that the people needed some entertainment, so one day a touring team showed up and after setting up a screen began to show Charlie Chaplin silent films. The looks on the faces of the spectators showed that any doubt in anyone's mind that the white men were magic was definitely dispelled. They were very amused but they had no idea of how a projector functioned and could not believe what they were seeing.

There was one wholesome form of entertainment that seemed to meet with enthusiastic approval and maybe the word entertainment is not appropriate because it was intended to be much more than that. It was actually very serious, but it was obvious that people enjoyed the periodic revival meetings held by the missionaries. I had never attended a revival meeting since that was not a part of the ritual of any church I had ever attended at home in Colorado, but revivals were very popular in parts of the country that most of the missionaries came from. Revivals served a very important function in rural areas of the South and the Midwest and people looked forward to those annual meetings when they would see friends and relations they had not seen for a long time.

The revivals were held on a hill across the valley about a mile away. There was lots of singing and much preaching culminating in a request for those who wanted to be saved to come forward and express their faith in the Lord Jesus Christ and their acceptance of Him as their Lord and Savior. It was an event that was most likely very effective since it drew very large crowds and I was told that sometimes a whole village would be converted en masse. I was particularly impressed by one of the preachers, an American who could be heard at least a mile away. The pressure of my work prevented me from attending the revivals myself but I could hear him clearly from where I was. There was no public address system so successful preaching sometimes required a powerful voice and I really did admire anyone who had such a talent. One of the missionaries told me that one man had been saved thirty-three times and I was properly impressed by that.

In our last year, we had a visit from an evangelist from the Methodist Mission in the Katanga who was on his way to take part in a revival somewhere else. He looked and talked like the evangelists we see on television today and when he preached he not only shouted but put on a great show with tears rolling down his cheeks. When no one was looking some of us referred to him as "Weeping Willie." We were told that since he was available there was going to be an impromptu revival so that everyone could take advantage of this opportunity to hear his message. The revival was going to be held on a weekday and it was expected of course that the students would be there.

I was not in favor of having the students miss a day of school so I called a meeting of the faculty. We met and after some discussion decided that the thing to do was hold classes as usual but let the students decide whether they wanted to attend classes or the revival. They had never been asked before to make such an important decision and it was apparent that their minds were in torment. They finally opted for classes and my stock went down another notch, but we felt that the boys would not benefit from such a meeting, while many of the villagers and mission employees would. As one of my professors used to say, if one misses a class there is a gap in his education that can never be filled. We felt that since the boys went to church three times on Sunday and had a sort of prayer meeting every morning that was sufficient exposure to the gospel. We reminded the organizers of the revival that we had a contract with the government to provide so many days of schooling a year and that it would not be honest to have them miss a day for a revival.

We did not get many visitors in the central Congo so we were always happy to welcome anyone who took the trouble. For a few days we enjoyed the presence of a bishop and his wife from what was then called a Negro church. They were interested in what we were doing and being of African ancestry they expected to relate to Africans and be accepted as brothers and sisters. But Africans, especially those in rural areas, consider anyone from outside their own tribe as a potential enemy and certainly as a foreigner, so they referred to the bishop as an usungu, the same word used for white people. The Africans were much less sensitive to skin color and had never experienced discrimination so they had other means of classifying people. In other words, the bishop and his wife were considered the same as white people because they came from America and had no more to do with Africa than the rest of us. The bishop's wife was very critical and was appalled at the primitive living conditions of the villages, specifically the way the women squatted on the ground to cook. She seemed to hold us responsible for not providing the women with chairs to sit on. If they had stayed longer she would have come to understand how the people lived and why they chose to live that way. Actually, the way the women, and the men as well, sat on their heels was very comfortable for those who were accustomed to it. For example, when they are herding cattle, cowboys do not usually carry along a chair and are accustomed to sitting on their heels just like the Africans. She did not notice that the villages were neat and clean and the people themselves, who bathed daily, were cleaner and better groomed than many people in the United States.

Before we went to the Congo our anthropology professor encouraged us to do some research while we were in Africa and I even bought a book entitled Notes and Queries in Anthropology, a guide to the sort of questions to ask and how to ask them. I never had the time to do any research among the uncontaminated segment of the population—those who did not speak French—and even if I had the time my knowledge of Otetela was inadequate for asking hard questions and understanding the response. Then too, I was just not interested in probing into the secret lives of the people. Such things are better left to the professionals. It was also futile for several reasons to ask those who did speak French. First of all, the motives of any foreigner were apt to be suspect. Then some of the questions would probably be considered impertinent and not worthy of a response if they touched upon personal subjects. Lastly, Africans, like people in other pre-industrial societies, tend to be outer-directed individuals so the responses would be worthless unless the interrogator was very clever. An outer-directed person is one who when replying to a question will give the answer he thinks the person wants to hear. It is not a matter of deliberately lying but a desire to please, a matter of courtesy. I found that I could get two different responses to the same question by the way the question was asked.

I learned a lot about the people and their customs by talking with the old-timers. One day one of the women who had been there for decades told me that when they first arrived she asked her cook if monkey meat was good and he replied that it was the next best thing to human flesh. She asked him if he had ever eaten a white person and he said no. She then told him he never should because it tastes terrible. In the early days when the missionaries were trying to learn the language they would point to some object and ask what it was. The answer was always the same and turned out to be the word for finger because the Batetela do not point with their finger but rather with their lips. It seemed strange but we learned to do it. To show how tall a child is an African would hold his hand with the palm up to show that the child was still growing and in the case of an animal his hand would be vertical with the thumb on top because an animal is longer than it is high.

CHAPTER 14

*History of the Congo and how it came
to be the Belgian Congo.*

ALTHOUGH THE AMERICAS had been discovered and colonized as early as the sixteenth century and trade with the Far East had flourished for centuries, Africa was still the Dark Continent until the late nineteenth century. There were strange and deadly diseases that made adventures in Africa dangerous, and the coast of West Africa was known for years as the white man's grave. The Portuguese were the first Europeans to have any contact with Africa, nibbling around the edges since the voyages of the Portuguese navigator Vasco da Gama, the first European to reach India by sea in 1499.

In 1502 he established Portuguese power in India and trading posts on the east coast of Africa as way stations on the route to India. Later, posts were established in Angola and at the mouth of the Congo River, named the Zaïre, about 1853, because they needed manpower to develop Brazil and the indigenous population there was not very cooperative. In collaboration with the Bakongo tribe they began to export thousands of slaves every year from the Congo to Brazil to work in the sugar cane fields.

The Arabs had been buying slaves along the east coast of Africa since the eighth century on a small scale. Their presence became much more important when the Sultan of Oman took over Zanzibar and much of the coast of Tanganyika in 1804, but most of the slave traffic was carried on in Zanzibar and the Sultan's influence did not extend very far inland at first. By 1840 the Arabs had opened a trading post at Tabora and some time later were able to push on to Nyangwe in the Manyema west of Lake Tanganyika. As the demand for ivory increased Zanzibar became more important as a port and a regular destination for ships from New England. An indication of its growing importance was the establishment there of an American consulate in 1836 and a British consulate in 1841.

Trade with the interior, including the Congo, was mostly in two commodities: ivory and slaves. Europeans and Americans were only interested in the ivory because the slave trade had been abolished in Europe early in the nineteenth century but the slave trade was flourishing in the countries to the east. Sometimes the slaves would be used as porters to carry the ivory since no other means of transport was available. It was a brutal business and many of the slaves died along the way because those who were weak or ill were left to die. Some of the slave caravans consisted entirely of women and children who were not strong enough to carry ivory but were captured simply to be sold as slaves in the Zanzibar slave market.

The most notorious slave trader was an Arab known as Tippu Tib who controlled all the slave trade in the upper Congo for about twenty years and was said to have had an army of several thousand men. One of his most important henchmen was a Mutetela, Ngongo Lutete, whose name has been spelled in various ways. Under his leadership, according to what I was told, the Batetela would raid villages of the neighboring tribes to capture the men to carry the ivory and the women and children to be sold as slaves. To discourage slaves from trying to escape they were sometimes fitted with heavy wooden collars to impede their movement or they would be yoked together in pairs by a pole with a yoke at each end.

Although they did not say so openly, our students seemed to be proud of their tribal ancestor, Ngongo Lutete, because he was the only ancestor of the tribe who is mentioned in the history books. He was also celebrated for his scientific research. The story was that when he was interested in the gestation process he had women in various stages of pregnancy brought before him and cut open while still alive so he could observe the development of the fetus. He also was reputed to enjoy crushing the skull of a baby with his bare hands. By some odd coincidence the same story with little if any difference was reported in James Michener's book *The Covenant* as being the custom of a chief, probably of the Matabele tribe in southern Africa.

Tippu Tib was engaged in what we consider a disgusting business but he was not completely bad. He was very helpful to all the European explorers who were moving through his territory and were at his mercy, providing them with information, helping them to find porters and offering them advice. Even though he sometimes had memory lapses concerning agreements made with the explorers his exceptional administrative ability was recognized and at one point he was considered for an important administrative post in the government of the Congo Free State.

The most illustrious of all the explorers was the Scottish missionary, Dr. David Livingstone, who first arrived in Africa in 1841 and spent much of the next thirty years exploring. He was the first white man to see Victoria Falls and the first to explore the Kwango and Kwilu regions and he was the first explorer to cross the continent from east to west when he went through Angola to Luanda on the Atlantic coast. He would have preferred to go down the Lualaba River, which he believed was the source of the Nile, but he could not obtain the canoes and porters he would have needed. As we shall see, it was just as well that he did not. He was also one of the best known explorers and when he had not been heard from for several years there was great concern in Britain and the United States.

James Gordon Bennett, publisher of the New York Herald, could recognize a good story when he saw one, so he sent his best foreign correspondent in the Middle East, Henry Morton Stanley, to find Livingstone. Stanley was one of the most extraordinary characters of the nineteenth century. Born in Wales and orphaned, he was put in what was called a workhouse, an institution described by Dickens in Oliver Twist, but he must have received a fairly good education. He left the work house while in his teens and came to American as cabin boy on a ship bound for New Orleans. There he was befriended by a merchant whose first and last names he took. He led an adventurous life, serving in both the Confederate and Union forces during the Civil War and traveling to the western frontier as a freelance journalist.

In 1864 he went west, first to St. Louis where he persuaded the editor of the Missouri Democrat to accept him as a contributor as he traveled all over the West, sending back dispatches as he went. Being very enterprising, he was also sending stories to the Herald on the side, looking to the future. He also worked as a bookkeeper and apprentice printer in Central City, and a gold miner and smelter laborer in Black Hawk, Colorado. In March, 1867 he was sent as a special correspondent to cover Major General Winfield Scott Hancock's expedition to pacify the plains Indians who objected to the invasion of their territory. During the next eight months Stanley firmly established himself in his new profession and became a foreign correspondent for the New York Herald.

On his first foreign assignment for the Herald he accompanied the British expeditionary force against Theodore II of Ethiopia. He also covered a civil war in Spain and in 1869 was sent to the Middle East where he remained for several years. Ordered to find Livingstone, Stanley set out from Zanzibar with a sizable expedition on March 21, 1871, and found Livingstone in the village of Ujiji on the eastern shore of Lake

Tanganyika, ill and nearly out of supplies. He greeted him with the memorable words, "Dr. Livingstone, I presume?" They became fast friends and when Stanley returned to Zanzibar he sent a generous shipment of supplies so that Livingstone could continue his explorations, but thirty years of tropical disease had taken their toll and Livingstone was dead within a year. One of his obsessions was finding the source of the Nile, a goal shared by other explorers such as Sir Richard Burton and John Speke. It was Speke who finally determined that the Nile did flow from Lake Victoria. Livingstone believed, quite logically, that the Lualaba, flowing north west of Lake Tanganyika, might be the source he was seeking. Stanley had promised Livingstone that he would return to Africa as soon as possible to carry on his work if Dr. Livingstone did not succeed. In 1874, three years after finding Livingstone, Stanley returned to Africa under the auspices of the New York Herald and the Daily Telegraph of London to fulfill his promise to Dr. Livingstone. He explored Lake Tanganyika and found that it had no connection with the Nile system. He then circumnavigated Lake Victoria and Lake Nyasa in a special boat he had built of Spanish cedar. Named the Lady Alice, it was built in eight five-foot sections, each light enough to be carried along narrow trails through brush and jungle. When assembled it had a beam of six feet and was two and one-half feet deep. With the help of Tippu Tib he assembled a party including three white men and 300 porters and headed down the Lualaba with a small fleet of dugout canoes, not knowing that north of the equator it would turn west, the eventually south and then west again. His 999-day expedition, which he described in his book *Through the Dark Continent,* tells of his explorations and the incredible voyage during which the party was often under attack from hostile natives and suffered severe hardships.

As they descended the Congo, which was an extension of the Lualaba, the natives seemed to regard their flotilla as a floating delicatessen. To cries of "Niama! Niama!" meaning meat! meat! accompanied by gestures clearly indicting their intention to eat their victims, canoes carrying hundreds of warriors were launched in their pursuit. Although the expedition only had thirty-four men capable of fighting they had Snider repeating rifles, some shotguns, and a machine gun which gave them enough of an advantage to assure their survival. When they arrived at Boma, a small trading post at the mouth of the Congo only 107 men and women and forty children remained of the original party. They had run out of food and trade goods and were in danger of starvation but were saved by the generosity of several European traders at Boma. Stanley realized the importance of his discovery but instead of returning directly to Europe he arranged for transportation of the remnants of his party back to Zanzibar on a ship of the Royal Navy and went with them to see that they were properly settled.

He went to London and tried to interest Queen Victoria in the Congo but she was already occupied, having enough to do with establishing a presence in territories in West Africa and Asia. He was also snubbed by the Royal Geographic Society; he was either American or Welsh, but not English so he did not deserve their attention. Europeans were scrambling to stake claims in Africa not necessarily for profit because the resources of Africa were unknown but for prestige. Considering the cost of building the infrastructure required to develop the colonies and open new markets for European products, hardly any of them were profitable in the long run. Britain had Nigeria, Gold Coast, the Gambia, Sierra Leone, and later Kenya and Uganda, which were quite enough to handle. France had a vast empire stretching from the Mediterranean to the equator, Germany wound up with Tanganyika, Southwest Africa, and Cameroon, and the Portuguese had Angola, Mozambique, and Portuguese Guinea. The only choice territory left and the one that later proved to have the greatest potential was the Congo.

King Léopold II of the Belgians was a frustrated imperialist with a tremendous ego who could not stand to be left out of the colonization he felt would give him more scope for the exercise of his talents than a small country like Belgium. After all, his cousins in some of the other countries were acquiring colonies and it was only fair that he should have one too. Belgium was a small country so force was out of the question but Léopold, being clever and determined, managed to find other means of reaching his goal.

In 1876 he convened in Brussels an international conference of geographers, explorers, and scientists and founded the International Association for the Exploration and Civilization of Central Africa. The Belgian committee was the most active and in 1878 and 1879 began to establish posts on Lake Tanganyika. He declared he had no territorial ambitions and assured everyone that his interests were purely scientific and humanitarian. That was actually the first step in a well conceived plan.

King Léopold was the only one to appreciate the importance of Stanley's discovery and when the Belgian committee was transformed into the Comité d'Etudes du Haut Congo he hired Stanley to expand the establishment of stations at the mouth of the Congo. He could not have made a better choice. Stanley was intelligent, resourceful, aggressive, and tough and knew the area better than anyone else. In 1879 Stanley entered the Congo from the Atlantic side, bringing with him steamboats to be used on the vast river system which made transportation in the interior much easier.

It was not possible to reach the interior by river from the sea because of the range of hills about 150 miles from the coast, so all the equipment, including the boats and their engines had to be dismantled and carried by porters from Matadi or Boma to Stanley Pool on the other side of the cataracts, as they are called. Then everything had to be put back together before it could be used. To put the project in perspective, try to imagine dismantling a Mississippi River steamboat and carrying it, piece by piece, from Pueblo to Denver, Colorado uphill all the way. Many of the porters were not as robust as they appeared to be and the loss of life was considerable. As soon as possible a railroad was built and conditions improved.

It was during that very difficult operation that Stanley received the name Bula Matadi, which meant rock crusher or someone with strength and perseverance. The named is usually spelled Bula Matari but since most Congolese have trouble with the sound of the letter r it is pronounced Matadi, like the name of the port. Other examples are the word crayon which is pronounced kidiyon and motor car, which is called a mutuka. When we were there all the Belgian administrators were referred to as the Bula Matadi. In 1880 the French, alarmed at Stanley's activities, sent out Savorgnan de Brazza to make treaties with the local chiefs north of the Congo River and establish French authority. He founded the city of Brazzaville and when he met Stanley at Stanley at Stanley Pool they agreed that everything north of the river would be French and everything south of the river would belong to Léopold. Then in 1882 the Comité d'Etudes du Haut Congo became the International Association of the Congo with trade as its main objective. Stanley made treaties with hundreds of local chiefs, treaties recognizing the authority and sovereignty of King Léopold. It is doubtful that the chiefs had any idea of what they were doing but it did provide a legal basis for the occupation as far as the Europeans were concerned. Stanley then opened trading posts throughout the country which formed the basis for the organization of a government.

The situation in Africa had become quite chaotic, so in 1885 the Berlin Conference on African Affairs was convened by Chancellor Otto von Bismarck and Jules Ferry, a Frenchman involved in colonization. Fourteen nations, including the United States, agreed to work for the suppression of slavery and the slave trade and declared complete liberty of commerce in the basin of the Congo and on the adjacent coasts. The claims of the various European nations were recognized and established. Among them was the Congo Free State which was being developed by King Léopold as his personal possession. Stanley had suspected that Léopold was trying to make the Congo a Belgian colony, but he did not suspect that the king's plan was even more audacious—to claim the entire territory of one million square miles as his personal domain.

Paying for the administration of such a large area, eighty-eight times the size of Belgium, was very expensive, so means were sought to generate some revenue. All ivory and rubber could only be sold to the state and in 1882 forced labor was introduced as a substitute for taxes in an effort to raise funds to support the administration. That was found to be necessary because it was not the custom of the indigenous population to work more than what was required for subsistence so there was no income from which taxes could be paid. There were many abuses which included physical punishment and in some cases mutilation. It was a frustrating situation for everyone concerned because the income from ivory and forest products could hardly have been sufficient. It was unfortunate that Léopold's agents did not know that the real wealth of the Congo lay not in the equatorial forest but in the mineral-rich Katanga in the southern part of the country.

One of the provisions of the Berlin Conference was that each of the colonial powers would undertake to eradicate the slave trade. Until 1892 neither the regime in the Congo Free State, nor the Germans who controlled Tanganyika had enough strength of oppose powerful slave traders such as Tippu Tib. It was the Germans who first took action against the slavers. In East Africa the Germans made a distinction between domestic slavery which they condoned as a necessary part of the social system, and the slave trade involving the exportation of slaves which they went after ruthlessly. At last the Arabs had come up against people prepared to be as merciless as they were.

In 1892 the Germans joined forces with the British to wipe out the slave trade in all of East Africa. At the same time the Congo Free State had become well enough established so that the king's men could take action against the slave trade west of Lake Tanganyika. That year full-scale war broke out between the Arabs under the command of Tippu Tib and the forces of the Congo Free State under the leadership of Baron Dhanis and Colonel Chaltin. There was a general uprising of the slave holders and slave traders but once the main centers of resistance at Nyangwe and Kasongo were captured their power was broken. Part of the rebellion of the Batetela was not suppressed until 1900.

Protests had begun in 1897 against the atrocities being committed and the methods of both state and private agents used to collect rubber were criticized. Then in 1903 large-scale agitation began, first in England and the United States, Germany, and other countries against the barbarous conditions in the Congo. The writing of journalist Edmund D. Morel and reports from missionaries and the British consul Sir Roger Casement, aroused great indignation. In 1904 King Léopold sent out a three-man commission to investigate. Its report was unfavorable and called for corrective action.

Léopold had exhausted his personal fortune and had borrowed heavily from the people of Belgium, so he was essentially bankrupt. His financial difficulties, combined with continued criticism of the policies of the Congo Free State, led him to offer the Congo to Belgium. In 1908, by act of the Belgian parliament, the Congo Free State was annexed to Belgium. That settled the king's debt and paved the way for serious reforms. Although the abuses which aroused so much indignation were not the work of the Belgian people or their government but were rather the work of Léopold's agents, the Belgians took their responsibility very seriously. They were determined to have a model colony and worked very hard to be the best colonialists.

Unlike the British, the French, the Portuguese, and the Spanish they had no tradition of colonialism or dreams of empire when the colony was thrust upon them. As a people they were not enthusiastic about having a colony but in a very logical manner they undertook to study the policies of the other colonial powers and came up with what they considered to be the most rational policy of all. It was all working quite well and the future of the Congo was very promising until independence was granted. It is ironic and very unfair that even today the Belgians are maligned because of a short period of misrule they were not even responsible for and which ended nearly 100 years ago, and their excellent record of enlightened colonialism is ignored.

CHAPTER 15

*What we thought of the Belgian administration.
The results of Jackie's efforts to improve the music
in the church. Things begin to fall apart. Our
departure and the trip home.*

I HAD TREMENDOUS RESPECT for the Belgian administration, with one possible exception. We had to pay duty on all our clothing and other necessities not available locally. We felt sometimes that the customs duties were unreasonable, but there was nothing we could do about it. We had learned that it is not wise to question the judgment of customs officials anywhere. As for the colonial administrators, they were impressive and I have never seen more hard working or dedicated people anywhere than in our area, Katako Kombe Territory, Sankuru District, Kasai Province. Our territorial headquarters was in Katako Kombe and the person we dealt with most was our territorial agent who lived just a few miles down the road.

He lived alone in a brick house with a thatched roof, was very friendly and spoke English as well as French, Flemish, and Swahili. He alone was responsible for maintaining law and order in an area as large as many American counties. He was the chief magistrate and had as his duties the taking of the census, collection of taxes, and everything else a local government had to do. He was a very busy man. Except for a few askaris, or native policemen, he was strictly on his own. The askaris were picturesque in their blue denim shirts and shorts, red fez, and black boots, and they were always from a different part of the country from the one in which they were serving.

They were respected but there was no sign that the people feared them. The only times I actually saw any of them in the performance of their duty was when one came to arrest someone for questioning who was involved in a civil suit. Serious violations of the law were handled in Katako Kombe.

Our local agent did not always have an automobile at his disposal and sometimes had to visit nearby villages on a bicycle. It was a very lean and efficient administration. He was Flemish, as were most of the colonial officers because the law required that they speak both French and Flemish and there were more Flemings willing to learn French than Walloons willing to learn Flemish. Cannibalism was supposed to have been wiped out long ago but our local Bula Matadi told me that every month he was asked to investigate the disappearance of half a dozen people. There was also the case of a chief who killed and ate a ten-year-old girl whose father was white in the belief that in so doing he would acquire some of the white man's yimba or vital force and magic. In his case it did not work because he was shot. The colonial officers, as far as I know, were incorruptible and set an example of honesty and efficiency that, unfortunately, was not followed after independence. They devoted much effort to improving the life of the people and protecting them from exploitation in many ways without disturbing their traditional culture any more than necessary.

When we entered our fourth year there was little change at the monitors school except that we did find another African teacher to take over the seventh-year classes. By then we no longer had any hope that there would be any improvement in the school facilities. One thing we did was start a library with books we collected. Many of them were in English but we did have a fair number of books in French for those who wanted to do recreational reading or acquire knowledge beyond what was in the school textbooks. We appointed a student as librarian to run the library but he was not very busy because the students and teachers did not have much intellectual curiosity and the habit of reading for pleasure had not yet been developed. The library would be there for those who wanted to use it and that was enough. An agreement was finally reached on the matter of teachers' salaries, which would be increased substantially each year until they reached parity with those of the government schools. It was not going to cost the mission anything because the government reimbursed the mission for all the expenses of the schools, including salaries. I was not familiar with the details because financial matters and dealing with the government were handled by the mission treasurer and the person who had been appointed school inspector. The only problem remaining was the difference between the income of the teachers and that of the local pastors and a solution to that must have been found. By that time I had lost interest in such difficulties because there was nothing I could do about them.

Our head teacher, Emile Luhahi, who had graduated from the secondary school on the Presbyterian mission, also left that year but did so with our blessing. A university had been founded in Elisabethville in 1955. It was open to anyone, European or African, who cold pass the entrance examination, but there was great emphasis on the insistence that it must have the same academic standards as the universities in Belgium. Luhahi was the most important individual in the school because of his loyalty and the continuity he provided, but he was ambitious as he should have been. His French was excellent but he needed further instruction in math and science, so the teachers who taught those subjects tutored him until he felt ready to take the examination.

He was one of fewer than twenty Congolese who passed, and after a preparatory year to make up for any deficiencies he was admitted to the university and there was no doubt that he was not in any way inferior to the white students. After graduation he was sent to Belgium on a full scholarship and finally received his doctorate. Naturally, we were very proud of him. We saw him several years later when he was taking some courses at the University of Denver and the last we heard he was president or chancellor of the University of Kisangani in the northeastern part of the Congo. The same year we sent one of our outstanding students to the Presbyterian mission to attend the college preparatory course there. I had to drive him down there myself and he was terrified at the thought of going into a different tribal area but he settled in and finished the course. Upon graduation he was sent to medical school in France on a French government scholarship and after completion of his studies he returned and was sent to Wembo Nyama by the government as the mission doctor. In a way that was the fulfillment of a dream because any time an expatriate could be replaced by a Congolese it meant that progress was being made. Unfortunately, that arrangement did not work out because there was a personality conflict between him and the American nurse who had known him as a student and he had to leave.

Some of the boys continued to make pottery, wicker furniture, and wood carvings for themselves or to sell for spending money. The pottery-making was a surprise because among the Batetela it was the women who made the pottery, but it seems to be true everywhere that if pottery is made by hand it is done by women and if a wheel is used it is made by men. The potter's wheel must have made the difference. The same thing seems to apply to sewing in countries where the sewing machine has been introduced.

I had learned silk screen printing in college, and when I saw supplies in one of the cities visited I had bought some. We had to cut the screens by hand, a tedious job requiring patience and precision but some of the boys were very good at it. We did not have any real use for it but we printed quotations from the Bible in Otetela on strips of paper the size of bumper stickers and put them on the trucks and buildings. Everyone seemed to find it a good idea.

Great progress had been made in the development of meaningful church music. Jackie finally introduced drums to accompany the choir and had some of the boys start writing their own hymns to produce religious music that was much more natural for them than what they had had before. When Martha was born she was unable to lead the choir for a few weeks and when she returned she found that under someone else's direction they had slipped back into their old ways. We were afraid that all her efforts had been wasted but we later learned that what she had taught them remained and became the standard for the future. A movement toward indigenous church music was taking hold all over the Congo and in other parts of Africa as well. One example was a Mass called the Missa Luba, written in the African idiom by and for the Baluba people.

She bought a dikembe, also called a mbira or thumb piano, and found it hard to play without practice. It was an interesting instrument. On a hollow rectangular box about ten inches long were eight strips of metal made of flattened bicycle spokes that could be plucked to make a sound. The spokes could be tuned by sliding them under the bar that held them to change the length. Sometimes a hollow gourd was used to increase the resonance. She joined the African Music Society based in South Africa and wrote articles for the society's journal. One was on the Batetela bamboo pipes, consisting of about eight pipes of one note each played by the students. Each one played his note at the right times and the result was a delightful melody. Other articles described trips taken to other villages and towns to put on concerts. The most extensive articles dealt with her work with Batetela church music.

Jackie did not have a driver's license. We did not have a car until we went to South Dakota and at that time no license was required there and it wasn't surprising to see boys as young as twelve driving tractors down the road. We did not have a car in Hartford or Brussels either, so she did not need one then. She did drive in the Congo but mostly just around the station or into the village where the shops were. Then one day one of the student nurses had to go to Yakusu, up near Stanleyville, to take some examinations so Jackie and the doctor's wife drove him to the Lomami River, two hours to the east. There he was met by a nurse from Tunda who then arranged for the trip north. It was the first time she had driven any distance alone and she was quite proud of her adventure. I asked her how she got along and she replied that there was really nothing to it. She had just followed the road.

One thing that seriously marred our last year in Ewangu was an indication of how the way of life we had known there was changing. During the first three years we had very little crime other than the boy stealing from our houses while we were in church, and that was not terribly important because very little was stolen. We had very few things of much value so it was not the financial loss that was significant but rather the loss of the feeling that everyone could be trusted. What really disturbed us was the discovery that our cook had been stealing from us for quite some time. The number of thefts had been increasing everywhere, but it had never occurred to us to suspect someone who was working in our own household. We were sorry we had to let him go, but we had no choice and he would not have expected otherwise.

About the same time there was suddenly a series of fires in the shops in the local shopping centers consisting of a few mud huts that sold items the local people needed, the most important being the pieces of cloth that made up the wardrobe of most of the women and some of the men. The shops were usually owned by either Portuguese or Belgians and managed by Congolese. Where they learned the scam was not clear but it worked like this. The store manager would remove most of the stock of cloth and other things and then set fire to the building, making sure that it was completely destroyed. He would then say that all had been lost in the fire but the reality was that it had been sold. The same sort of fraud is not unknown in more advanced countries. There was no way of insuring those small shops so the result was that financing one in the bush became a much less attractive investment.

Every month I would receive money from the treasurer to buy food for the students, to pay the workmen, and pay any other school expenses. I kept the cash in one drawer of the filing cabinet that had a lock. The lock was merely symbolic because the metal was so thin that it would not discourage a serious thief but it had always been adequate. One day I found that someone had pried open the drawer and had stolen some of the money. Fortunately, he had been careless or in a hurry because when he reached in he only got part of the money that was there. I was upset because the money was to be used to buy food for the boys, including meat for Sunday dinner. I felt that the students probably knew who had stolen the money or could find out, so I explained to them that I would appreciate their help in finding the thief because there would be no money to buy meat until the money was recovered. For two Sundays there was no meat and no progress in finding the culprit. I considered calling in a witch doctor to find the thief but I was told that such a recourse would not be acceptable. It was easy to see why that would not be a good idea because we were not supposed to believe in that sort of thing. Then too there was a possibility that the thief did not either and would not return the money.

After the second meatless Sunday the entire student body came to my house in a demonstration to protest the ban on meat. They appeared to be rather menacing and I wished that someone in a position of authority like the station pastor or one of the senior missionaries would come and talk to the students, but no one came and I was left to face them alone. In such a situation it was best not to show any sign of weakness, which would have undermined my authority, so I did my best to appear confident and in control, explaining that the school was on a limited budget and when there was no money we could not buy meat. I tried to explain that it was their money that had been stolen, and it was in a sense, but that was an argument they could not accept because they believed we had access to unlimited funds and that I was being unfair. They finally went away. They had meat the next Sunday and the money was never found. It was after that incident that they began to call me Bwana instead of Uwandji, Bwana being the Swahili word for chief. I thought it was because I had become more irascible than usual but someone told me that it was a mark of respect for a person who had shown strength or courage. I had not given in and they got what they wanted so everyone was satisfied and no one lost face.

We thought about the event and felt that if they did not care about the school, why should we? Actually, it was unrealistic to expect that much loyalty to an institution that was not of their own creation. I also remembered a young architect we had met in Hartford who was going to India to design and build something for a mission society. He had said that if at the end of his tour he had not trained someone to take his place he would think he had failed. I mentioned that to Jackie, saying that I had come out there to impart certain skills and knowledge like French, geography, and art, and now that there were several people who could do that as well as I could there was no reason for me to come back to spend another four years in an atmosphere which was less than congenial. She said she felt much the same way about the music and other things she had taught and that coming back would put off the responsibility of her students to apply what they had learned. I remembered too that the bishop had said something about working ourselves out of a job.

When Hari came home from boarding school he and Paul spent most of their time building things, sometimes with the help of the artisans at the school. They made some improvements on the house they had built by the wash shed and they built a small car like the ones in the soap box derby and also a covered wagon. They usually went down to the pond behind the house for a swim every day and except for the time they were caught smoking homemade cigarettes with some of the other boys all their activities were constructive.

Our Belgian agriculture teacher had come out for only three years so he left and was replaced by an American. We were fond of Fernand and missed him after he left. He had done a fine job in many ways that could make life better for the people of that region if they cared to take advantage of what he had taught them. The new agriculture teacher was well trained and would bring a new approach to some of the problems, expanding on what had already been accomplished.

Our daughter was born in December and was doing very well. Jackie gave up some of her activities because nothing was more important than taking care of the new baby. We borrowed a baby carriage and every day Jackie would take her for a walk. She seemed to thrive on the formula made from powdered milk imported from the United States. Big corporations like Nestlé and Borden were trying to expand into the African market so there was plenty of dried milk available. For the Africans it was not so good because they did not understand that the water had to be boiled and thousands of babies died before protests caused the companies promoting the milk to reconsider their policy. Martha's birth certificate was printed in both French and Flemish and we also had her birth registered with the American consulate so she would have an American birth certificate.

We started to make plans for our return about six months before we were due to leave. We had no suitable wardrobe for the trip and it took so long for things to arrive from home that we got our orders in early. I had my mother send me some shirts and slacks and enough clothes for the boys to make them presentable. For Jackie the question of what to wear was more serious. She saw a dress in a Lord and Taylor ad in the New Yorker and ordered it. That was certainly the best solution because she could not arrive in New York looking like she had just spent four year in the bush. I bought a pair of leather shoes in Luluabourg because the brown sneakers I was accustomed to wearing would not project a suitable image outside the Congo. We decided to wait until we got to London for any important purchases. It was summer so we did not need any heavy clothing.

We had very little access to news other than the BBC and did not pay much attention to what was going on in the rest of the country or the world. It was only later that we found out there had been quite a bit of political activity and agitation for independence while we were there. The proponents of independence, usually supported and encouraged by outside interests, saw an opportunity to seize power for themselves. The same thing was happening throughout Africa. Unscrupulous individuals, encouraged by well-meaning but ignorant people in Europe and America who had the idea that Africans were suffering under the yoke of colonialism, campaigned in the name of freedom and democracy but had quite a different agenda. The colonial governments offered very little resistance because colonialism was no longer in fashion and the colonies had become more of a burden than an asset. It was only when independence was achieved that the people began to understand the meaning of oppression. Honest and efficient government was replaced by massive inefficiency and pervasive graft and corruption with devastating effect on the economy.

That was less true in the former French colonies, but that is another story.

The Belgian people, on the whole, never wanted the colonies so there was no resistance at all and the consensus was that the colonies were not worth one drop of Belgian blood. There were colonies because after World War I Belgium took over the administration of two former German colonies, Ruanda and Urundi. Independence was granted with an understanding that there would be a gradual transfer of power with Belgian administrators staying on as advisors. The first president, Patrice Lumumba, was a Mutetela who had been expelled from the monitors school before we arrived. As soon as he became president in 1960 he ignored the agreements and made decisions that many feel plunged the country into chaos.

The time finally came for us to start our preparations for our trip home. We began to pack up the few things we wanted to take home and when I started going through the books in the bookcase I found that the termites had come through the wall and had started on the books. As much as half an inch was missing from all the pages of some of them.

When the school year ended we had a graduation ceremony to which I wore my linen suit, the one that looked like I had slept in it five minutes after I had put it on. Then we invited the whole graduating class and the teachers to our house for a spaghetti dinner. It was a gala affair and probably the first time most of the students had enjoyed Italian food. Just a few days before we left there was another visitation from all the students in a body but the mood was quite different. It was very friendly and the purpose was to plead with us to come back. I had said nothing to indicate that we were not planning to come back but, as I have said, Africans are very perceptive and they knew we had several reasons for not returning. We were touched that they wanted us back, but considering what happened when independence was granted three years later we made the right decision. Africans are not the only ones who are intuitive.

Our original plan was to take the train from Luluabourg to Elisabethville, then through the Rhodesias and Bechuanaland and South Africa to Capetown. I have always liked traveling by train, being able to observe the landscape, to get up and move around and be lulled to sleep at night by the rhythm of the wheels. There is something romantic about trains that aircraft lack. The Orient Express evokes all kinds of exotic images and railroads have been the subject of many songs, such as "The Wabash Cannonball," the "Chattanooga Choo-Choo," and the "Atchison, Topeka and Santa Fe." No one has, as far as I know, been inspired to write a song by the sight of the flight attendants pushing the drinks cart up the aisle on a noisy Boeing 737. From Capetown we would have taken a ship to England and then either another ship or a plane to New York. The Board of Missions had a very generous policy concerning travel home at the end of a tour. It did not matter how long the trip took and how much it cost, within reason, because the board felt anyone who had been in Africa for four years deserved a vacation.

It would have been a wonderful trip, very restful, but because of Rosebud we decided it would be more prudent to fly, so we were driven to Lodja where a landing strip had been prepared by removing the brush and leveling a strip about 3,000 feet long, enough for a DC-3 that came in from Léopoldville once a week. The terminal building was a small metal shack instead of a grand terminal with a duty-free shop and the parking was free. After having our passports renewed at the American consulate in Léopoldville we proceeded to Brussels on a Sabena DC-7. On the plane there was an interesting arrangement for our daughter. The stewardess slung a sort of hammock from the overhead baggage compartment and Martha slept almost the entire trip.

We stayed in Brussels a few days to become accustomed to the climate change. The first evening we were wandering around downtown enjoying the sights when we realized that we were getting hungry. We looked at our watches and discovered that it was after nine o'clock and it was still light. We were so used to seeing a large orange ball sink below the horizon so quickly at exactly six o'clock that we could watch its progress and had forgotten that such as thing as twilight existed.

We then went to London and had an interesting and pleasant vacation. We were staying in an old hotel on the north edge of London that was only for foreign missionaries and had been recommended by some British friends. Our accommodations were austere but comfortable, with the bathroom down the hall as was customary at the time the hotel was built. In a way it was more like a boarding house because three meals a day plus morning and afternoon tea were included in the price. The food was plain but well prepared and we particularly enjoyed the sumptuous English breakfasts served in the best English tradition with porridge, bacon or ham and eggs, sausage, toast, and coffee or tea. We did miss having a large papaya. We took the number 19 bus downtown to Picadilly Circus and went on a shopping spree on Regent Street, buying such necessities as wool skirts and sweaters and tweed jackets.

We went to the British Museum to see the African sculpture and all the other wonderful art objects. I met the keeper of African art, a man who had written some of the finest books on African sculpture. He was very hospitable. I showed him several small fetishes I had brought with me and he showed me some of the art from the Congo that was not on display. He took me to lunch but our conversation was cut short because I began to have an attack of malaria and had to go back to the hotel and rest. We also went to Oxford and had lunch in a very elegant restaurant, surrounded by what must have been the cream of British intellectuals. In London we did lots of walking because almost everything was farther away than it looked on the map. We saw the Tower of London, Windsor Castle, and Buckingham Palace, where we watched the changing of the guard and took pictures of the boys in front of the guards with their bearskin hats. We also went to the zoo where we saw the penguins and many other animals and Paul got to ride on a camel. We had always heard that the English were cold and unfriendly but everywhere we went people were courteous and helpful. We had bought some books and did not have room for them in our luggage so I went into a stationery shop to buy some paper and string so we could mail them. The shopkeeper took the books, wrapped them neatly and returned them to me saying there was no charge.

We wanted to see something outside of London so we rented a small car and took a short trip. We had no idea where we were going but it did not matter. We headed southwest and were impressed with how neat, clean, and orderly everything was. We spent the night in a bed and breakfast place and then drove back to London the next day. The woman who had said that I could pass for a Scot must have been right because the next day I was standing on the pavement, which is what the British call the sidewalk, in my new Scottish tweed jacket when someone stopped and asked for directions. I could pass for a native as long as I kept my mouth shut.

We flew to New York and went to the office of the Board of Missions. I told the personnel secretary that we would not be going back to the Congo and he simply replied that he was not surprised. We tried to reserve tickets on the train to Denver but were unable to do so because while we were away a decision had been made to gradually phase out all passenger service on the railroads. Whether we liked it or not we had to go by air, or take the bus, which would have been worse. We finally arrived back in Denver, glad to be home and wondering what to do next.